How Journalists Use Twitter

How Journalists Use Twitter

The Changing Landscape of U.S. Newsrooms

Alecia Swasy

LEXINGTON BOOKS
Lanham • Boulder • New York • London

Published by Lexington Books
An imprint of The Rowman & Littlefield Publishing Group, Inc.
4501 Forbes Boulevard, Suite 200, Lanham, Maryland 20706
www.rowman.com

Unit A, Whitacre Mews, 26-34 Stannary Street, London SE11 4AB

British Library Cataloguing in Publication Information Available

Library of Congress Cataloging-in-Publication Data

Library of Congress Cataloging-in-Publication Data Available

ISBN 978-1-4985-3218-1 (cloth : alk. paper)
ISBN 978-1-4985-3219-8 (electronic)

Printed in the United States of America

For Sue and Dean Mills. Thanks for cheering me
on for more than three decades.

In memory of Ben E. Hill, Jr. You live on in our laughter.

Contents

Acknowledgments

This book would be a total bore without the candor from so many dedicated journalists at the four newspapers. Thanks to all who took time out to chat and welcome me to their newsrooms. It reminded me why I love journalism and now teach—to instill the best practices, fire in the belly and devotion to democracy—to tomorrow's journalists. A special thanks to Kevin Riley, at the *AJC*, Ryan Rusak at the *News*, Linda Shapley and Dan Petty at the *Post* and Paul Tash at the *Times*.

Research requires a lot of time and help from anyone willing to pitch in, plus a strong network of family and friends to cheer you on. I am blessed to be surrounded by dozens of people who did all of that while I worked on this book.

The research began while I was working on my Ph.D. at the Missouri School of Journalism. A team set out to study how Twitter was used by newspaper readers watching the 2012 Presidential Debates. As a journalist-turned-academic, I was watching a big change in how the news media covered politics, thanks to this relatively young service called Twitter. I was fortunate to explore this during my research hours working for the Reynolds Journalism Institute. Thanks to the Donald W. Reynolds Foundation and Randy Picht at RJI for providing funds so I could visit three newsrooms for my interviews.

Ph.D. students spend a lot of time digging for things, but I was a newcomer to academic hunting expeditions. I learned that a graduate student's best friends are the research goddesses Dorothy Carner and Sue Schuermann at Journalism library. Thanks for your dedication to helping students.

Ditto for the academic advisors, staff and faculty of the school. Martha Pickens and Sarah Smith-Frigerio keep the place running smoothly, fielding every question for masters and doctoral students. Likewise, I am so grateful for the many professors who guided me from day one. George Kennedy, Yong Volz, Charles Davis, and Stephanie Craft, among others, were always ready to help answer questions or provide encouragement. A special thanks to Randy and Joyce Smith, two wonderful mentors and friends.

This dissertation was enhanced by the guidance of a great committee, led by Yong Volz. She is a tireless mentor and coach, offering precise and fast feedback on my research. As a professor, she cares deeply about training future professors. She is a role model for all of us. Thanks to

Mitchell McKinney, Ryan Thomas, Tim Vos, and Dean Mills for their time, feedback, and encouragement as my dissertation committee. And thanks to Nicolette Amstutz, Kasey Beduhn, and Jimmy Hamill at Lexington Books/Rowman & Littlefield for lots of help on the book's production.

No one could survive the rigor of a Ph.D. program without a strong personal network of family and friends. I am truly blessed with seven siblings and the extended families beyond them. Hardly a day went by without a call, card or email from one of them. My mother, Maribel Allison Swasy, is the definition of strength and grace. She is one of the funniest and sweetest people on the planet. Thank you for being my number one fan.

Finally, this dissertation is dedicated to three very special people. Dean and Sue Mills have been my adopted family for over 33 years, dating back to my undergraduate years at Penn State. Dean has been a precise editor, starting with my undergraduate classwork, my two previous books and this project. I look forward to his sharp eye as I pursue more books in the future. Sue is a dear friend and second mama always ready to share a tasty stir fry and conversation.

The dedication is shared with my late brother-in-law, Ben Hill. You live on in our laughter and retelling of many stories of happy times. We love and miss you.

Introduction

The *Denver Post's* online night producer was about to go home when he made one last check of his Twitter account at about 1 a.m., July 20, 2012. The tweet said multiple gunshots had been fired at a movie theater in Aurora, Colorado. The night editor called the metro editor and others to get back to work, allowing the *Post* to quickly get a story on its website and in the morning newspaper. Twelve people were killed and dozens more injured in the theater shooting, one of the deadliest rampages in U.S. history.

"If the night producer hadn't checked Twitter, we would've been way behind," said Dan Petty, social media editor at the *Post*. (D. Petty, personal communication, April 11, 2014). Likewise, when the *Post* wanted to find local runners after the Boston Marathon bombings, editors scanned Twitter to see who had crossed the finish line and who remained on the course. "Twitter will always be faster," Petty said. "You can have a newsroom of 200 people, but we can't compete with hundreds of people at the finish line" (Swasy & Wolfgang, 2013).

Twitter, which has grown into a dominant force in social media circles, is now influencing the practices inside newsrooms like the *Denver Post*. Founded by four friends in 2006, Twitter started because four "lonely people came together to build a product designed to connect them to each other and the world around them" (Honan, 2013, p. 1). It was started as a plaything so friends could tell one another what they were doing, whether it's eating a sandwich or watching the Oscars. Limited to just 140 characters, a tweet was a fast, shorter version of email that could be posted for a broader audience.

Twitter has emerged as a respected source of information, not just a purely social platform where friends share photos, videos and snippets of information. Tweeters want to know what's going on and they want to share it with others, making it more of an information distillery that helps users avoid information overload (Johnson & Yang, 2009). Twitter reports that it has more than 200 million people tweeting 400 million times a day (Tsukayama, 2013).

Indeed, Twitter has become a powerful communications tool. Marketers use it to promote new products or to do instant surveys of consumers. Hollywood celebrities hire public relations firms to build their Twitter following because it increases their paychecks if they are seen as having a large posse. Technology writers figured Twitter could be the next flash that fizzles, like MySpace or other web startups. But its roots are getting deep. "The history of the Internet suggests that there have been cool Web sites that go in and out of fashion and then there have been open standards that become plumbing," said Steven Johnson, author and technology observer. "Twitter is looking more and more like plumbing, and plumbing is eternal" (Carr, 2010, p. 1).

Meanwhile, 23 percent of those who use a social network such as Twitter or Facebook are now getting their daily news from those sites. According to Pew Research Center, nearly one-in-10 U.S. adults get news through Twitter (Mitchell, 2013). "Twitter has become a true global town square—a public place to hear the latest news, exchange ideas and connect with people all in real time," wrote Twitter's editorial director Karen Wickre, in a company memo (Tsukayama, 2013).

As news organizations struggle to attract and retain customers, many believe that they must figure out a way to integrate these social media platforms into their daily habits and routines if they are going to successfully lead readers to the original newspaper or website for content. Specifically, given Twitter's role as an information distillery, many scholars, editors and publishers want to know how Twitter can be incorporated into the routines of newsgathering, reader engagement and promotion of their products (Ahmad, 2010, Barnard, 2012). To be sure, Twitter does raise concerns. Singer (2010) found newsroom editors fear using information from Twitter because outsiders can easily alter photos before tweeting them. Another concern is the use of social media platforms to spread inaccurate information to further their pet causes.

Despite some concerns, Twitter is changing newsroom cultures and practices (Greer & Yan, 2010). Drawing on the diffusion of innovations and boundary theories, as well as the concept of social capital and agenda setting, this book analyzes the introduction, adoption, and institutionalization of Twitter in U.S. newspapers.

Diffusion of innovation theory (Rogers, 1962) helps explain the process of adoption of technological breakthroughs by individuals and organizations. Rogers defined innovation as an idea, practice, and object that is considered new. Boundary theory is used to first explain the traditional newsroom structure and hierarchies in order to understand how a new technology such as Twitter shifts those boundaries. For instance, social media makes news a 24/7 event and dictates that reporters now respond to more events, not just those they choose to cover on a traditional beat.

Social capital theory is applied to explain how Twitter can enhance a journalist's standing in a community and translate that into economic gains. Capital takes three forms: Economic capital, which is anything that can be converted into money or other tangible things, such as property rights. The second form is cultural capital, which can take the form of an advanced education, the sum of knowledge, and which helps people enhance their positions in a society. The third form is social capital, which is made up of social obligations or connections (Bourdieu, 1986). Social capital is what a person gains by participating in a community, whether geographically-located such as a church or virtually situated such as Facebook. Agenda setting theory examines the issue of how the media decide what becomes prominent in each day's news coverage (McCombs, 1972).

Diffusion of innovations and social capital theory together can help us understand how journalists in metropolitan newspapers are adopting Twitter as a new technology and how the use of the social media platform helps them each develop and build their capital, such as getting a better job or greater recognition from their bosses. In turn, these theories help explain how the news organizations are adopting Twitter to improve their standing in the communities they serve. Agenda setting theory applies because it shows how new, outside voices on Twitter are now being weighed in deciding what gets covered in each news cycle.

To explore these issues, 50 journalists at four metropolitan newspapers—the *Atlanta Journal-Constitution*, the *Dallas Morning News*, the *Denver Post* and the *Tampa Bay Times*—were interviewed from March to June 2014. Journalists shared their experiences testing and adopting Twitter into their daily routines, how Twitter has changed their news gathering techniques and how the overall news organizations are trying to use Twitter to improve traffic to their websites.

ONE

Using Theory to Understand Twitter

To understand a new innovation, it's helpful to look to the past for clues on what makes a product a breakthrough or a bomb. Communications scholars have learned a lot by studying a theory that began in a cornfield.

Diffusion of innovations theory helps explain the process of adoption of technological breakthroughs by individuals and organizations. Everett Rogers (1962) defined innovation as an idea, practice and object that is considered new.

> Diffusion is a kind of social change, defined as the process by which alteration occurs in the structure and function of a social system. When new ideas are invented, diffused, and are adopted or rejected, leading to certain consequences, social change occurs. (Rogers, 1962, p. 6)

Rogers trained as a rural sociologist, but drew upon other disciplines such as anthropology and education to develop his theory. His earliest studies focused on agriculture, specifically how Midwestern farmers heard about, then tested a new kind of hybrid corn seed on their farms. In 1971, Rogers updated his theory by using it to evaluate social systems. Rogers described innovation as a process where the new idea, technology or other breakthrough is shared through certain channels over time among members of the same social system. It can be broken down into the four separate components that influence the scope and speed of the diffusion: 1) What is nature of the innovation? 2) What is the influence of the social system on adopting the innovation? 3) What are the communications channels used to spread the innovation? And 4) How much time is required for the innovation to be adopted?

NATURE OF THE INNOVATION

Rogers outlined an additional five more technical determinants of innovation that will determine whether the innovation is adopted or rejected
in the context of the social system and communications channels. They
are: 1) relative advantage over existing innovations; 2) Compatibility to
existing work routines; 3) Complexity of the innovation; 4) Trialability, or
is it easy to experiment with the innovation? And 5) Observability, or
how visible is it to colleagues and bosses?

In this case, the innovation being studied is Twitter. It is a technological change because it is a new way to gather and disseminate information
from people around the globe. Historically, journalists have had to cope
with other seismic technological changes in how they do their jobs, with
each one seeming to be both frightening and promising at the same time.
Consider the invention of the telegraph. The telegraph was first used in
the 1840s and newspapers, eager to spread information, encouraged the
development of the first experimental line between Baltimore and Washington (Schudson, 1978).

> The (Baltimore) *Sun's* early use of (the telegraph) encouraged wider
> acceptance of telegraphic communication, although most of the press,
> like most of the public, was at first unwilling to believe, or unable to
> comprehend its promise. (Taylor, 1951, p. 152)

Likewise, the arrival of radio was met with skepticism and concern about
whether audiences would tolerate advertising messages in between relig-
ious and news programming. But a 1929 survey by a professor at the
Massachusetts Institute of Technology found that one-third of U.S. homes
had radios, which meant the potential audience was 41.4 million people,
80 percent of them listening to it every day. Newspapers tried to block
radio station's access to wire services, but they failed and radio became a
major force in airing news, such as the trial of the Lindbergh baby kid-
napper in 1934 (Marquis, 1984).

Television, in turn, made its mark when big news happened, such as
the assassination of President John F. Kennedy in November 1963. The
nation collectively grieved when Walter Cronkite "put on his horn-
rimmed glasses to glance at a message from Dallas, and then, blinking
back tears, told his viewers that their leader was gone" (Gillmor, 2004).

The advent of one information technology after another has continued
to reshape the communications industry.

> The invention of the audiocassette by Philips in 1962 put an easy-to-use
> recordable audio format in the hands of almost everyone. The develop-
> ment of the Beta format by Sony put a similar video format in the
> hands of millions. The subsequent development of VHS . . . made video
> commonplace . . . These technologies flourished for two reasons: (1)
> The format became standardized, and (2) the new technology was sim-

pler to use. So it is with the (World Wide) Web. (Crossman, 1997, p. 20-21)

With the explosion of the Internet and a variety of services such as Yahoo and Google, communications was made easier with email. Gillmor (2004) describes it as the "first draft of history" was now being partially written by the former audience, thanks to a variety of online publishing tools. Now, social media platforms such as Facebook and Twitter have taken it to a new level of public and searchable exchanges. Email is limited to a person's list of professional and personal contacts. Twitter allows users to search all Twitter accounts for a broad range of topics of interest, such as news on Iraq or a restaurant review. Twitter allows complete strangers to get acquainted. Unlike email or telephone calls, Twitter is open to the public to join any conversation.

This expands the platform into a new kind of public sphere where anyone can exchange ideas, a key part of democracy (Craft & Davis, 2013). Habermas (1989) defined the public sphere as society engaged in public debate. All citizens have access to this sphere and can talk without any interference. Anyone with access to the Internet can use Twitter because it is free, thus making it an open forum. Indeed, the only limitation is users must keep their messages, or "tweets" to 140 characters or less. As Gillmor (2004) pointed out about the Internet, these exchanges are a shift from the one-way conversation with readers because the former audience can now join or even start the conversation. The explosion of smart phones and social media such as Facebook and Twitter allow consumers to customize their own news sites and focus on the content they want to read (Dahlgren, 2009). Unlike posting a comment on a news organization's website, Twitter users decide what to promote as content, rather than just reacting to what a newspaper has posted to its website. The instantaneous nature of tweets has accelerated the give and take of two-way communications between the public and the media because reporters and the public are more mobile with smart phones, rather than being tethered to a desktop computer.

In summary, Twitter is a technological innovation—much like the telegraph and television in previous generations—because it is a new platform for gathering and spreading information around the globe. It provides open access for the exchange of ideas to anyone who has access to the Internet, thus creating a new public sphere for multiple conversations, not just one-sided transmission of news by traditional newspapers. Anyone is now a publisher because digital technology allows all to distribute what they consider to be newsworthy.

SOCIAL SYSTEM FOR DIFFUSION OF INNOVATION

The next determinant of innovation is the social system through which the innovation has been introduced. For instance, a social system is a group of people who share a common goal, such as members of a Methodist church share a collective belief in the Protestant worship of God, or a high school where students all cheer for their football team.

In the case of a newsroom, the social system is a group of reporters and editors who are united in the same goal: cover the news and publish it in a timely fashion. Senior editors and the publisher set the broad agenda for news coverage so it fits within the budget, which influences the social system of the newsroom. Singer, Hermida, et al (2011) determined that three resources determine newsroom practices: time, space and staff. There are also opinion leaders, such as popular columnists or investigative journalists, who wield influence because they serve as a face of the newsroom's best work. Indeed, one of the core values of journalists is to investigate for the truth and to give context in the explosion of so many information sources (Weaver, et al., 2007). The social system of a newsroom varies depending on the size—larger papers such as the *New York Times* have more layers of senior editors, managing editors, department editors, copy editors, designers and reporters. This reflects the big newspapers' greater circulation and revenues from a broader variety of advertisers, which give them more resources to cover everything from international news to the New York suburbs. Weekly newspapers operate at the other end of the spectrum, relying on very small budgets generated from very local advertisers in their hometowns, and employing one editor and a handful of freelancers.

Rogers (1962) believed that his research on the diffusion of innovations has played an important role in helping put social structure back in the communication process. This makes sense because the adoption of an innovation requires that it be easy to use, experiment with, and implement.

At the most elite newspapers, such as the *New York Times* and the *Washington Post,* senior editors have far greater resources to appoint special teams to investigate and implement new innovations, such as Twitter, and employ trainers to teach the staff how to most effectively use the innovation. By doing this, those newsrooms have more flexibility to try out new innovations. In smaller newsrooms, however, embracing a new social media platform may fall low on the list of priorities when there are so few staffers employed to do everything from cover the police beat to delivering the paper.

COMMUNICATION CHANNELS

The communications channels, as defined by Rogers (1983), rely on people teaching others about new innovations. Diffusion requires a certain amount of "heterophily" or differences among people. If two people are completely alike in their knowledge of the innovation, no diffusion can occur because both are already aware of it (Rogers, 1983). In the case of a Methodist church, established elders of the church teach newcomers through church bulletins, Bible study, Sunday worship and Sunday school. In the case of newsrooms, little has changed since Breed (1955) wrote about how new staffers learn the ropes in a newsroom: they read the paper and use it as a model for what they write. Editors coach them on their mistakes.

> The typical conference consists of two persons, the reporter and the city editor and can amount to no more than a few words. (Reporter: "One hurt in an auto accident uptown." City editor: "Okay. Keep it short.") . . . the staff cooperates on a job they all like and respect: getting the news. The newsroom is a friendly, first-namish place (p. 330).

The communications channels in the process of adopting Twitter includes informal conversations among reporters, memos from senior management on how to use Twitter and emails among reporters and their colleagues at competing publications. These relationships rely on people and their intangible capital, such as their creativity, knowledge, and abilities, to help the innovation take hold.

SPEED OF DIFFUSION

The final determinant is the amount of time required for the innovation to be adopted. In the case of Twitter, some reporters who are already active via personal accounts on Facebook or Twitter may be the early adopters of the innovation in the workplace. Others might be slower to buy into the idea because they view sending out multiple tweets a day as just another chore on their "To Do" list.

Studying the diffusion of an innovation varies by industry because processes vary by the complexity of the project. For instance, automakers come out with new cars just once a year, while most newspapers publish daily and update their websites throughout the day. Likewise, Rogers was able to judge the results of farmers planting a new type of corn seed within months because it takes one summer to judge if the corn crop is more bountiful than previous yields. But Rogers found that diffusion of new technologies, such as the radio and television, took years. It took nearly 20 years before television reached 95 percent of U.S. households, while the telephone took more than 80 years to reach that level of homes

(Rogers, 2003). In contrast, before Rogers died in 2004, he observed: "The Internet has spread more rapidly than any other technological innovation in the history of mankind (Rogers, 2003, p. xix).

Application of DOI in Newsroom Studies

To understand Twitter's adoption, it is helpful to look at what other scholars have done with diffusion of innovation theory and the study of other newsroom practices. Many scholars have used Rogers's theory to study how newsrooms adopt new innovations (Singer, 2004, Garrison, 2000, 2001, Duhe & Mortimer, 2004, Dailey, Demo, & Spillman, 2005). Some scholars focused on different concepts of diffusion of innovation theory, while others studied it by employing different methods, such as surveys or interviews with journalists.

Singer (2004) used diffusion of innovations theory in her study of four newspapers that had converged their operations with a local television station. In doing so, two once-competing news companies deepen their news reports and save money. Singer structured her research questions to address the five characteristics of Rogers' theory on the adoption of innovations: relative advantage, compatibility, complexity, trialability and observability of newsroom convergence. Journalists in several news-rooms were interviewed and then asked to complete a questionnaire about convergence. Singer found the first example of a relative advantage was reporters believed working in a new medium, such as television or online, instead of just producing a print newspaper, was a boost to their own careers. The second relative advantage Singer found was journalists believed working in a converged newsroom made them better storytell-ers because they now had three outlets for their work—print, television and the website. Singer found one complexity was general fear of learn-ing new media formats. But as reporters learned those skills, those fears seemed to ease. A complexity issue that was universal was the lack of time to produce more products for more media outlets. Taking time to gather video or photos meant a print reporter had less free time to roam City Hall talking to sources and finding news.

Singer concluded the newsrooms would be successful at convergence, especially as staffers grow more comfortable with their new tasks. Since that study, other scholars have come to similar conclusions. Duhe & Mor-timer (2004) found that nine of 10 television newsrooms were practicing some form of convergence with partner news organizations. The majority of the newsrooms said they shared content with their convergence part-ners. The partners gave priority to producing content for each of their websites, radio reports and newspaper stories. About 90 percent of those surveyed deemed the convergence experience as positive. The major problem cited was the increased pressure on journalists to turn out more stories for more media outlets.

Garrison (2001) used diffusion of innovation theory to study the adoption of online information technologies at newspapers over a six-year period starting in 1994. The research used a questionnaire to ask editors at 500 or more newspapers about their use of the Internet and specific services such as Dow Jones, Lexis-Nexis, or America Online. Some of Rogers's five features were tested, such as measuring rate of adoption of online resources over the six-year period. To do this, the questionnaires asked how often—daily, weekly, etc.—reporters used the online services. Garrison found that adoption of the innovation was nearly complete at the end of the six years. One of the relative advantages that Garrison found was reporters and editors were doing more of their own research as compared to asking librarians to do it for them. In 1995, fewer than one in four reporters conducted online research. By 1999, that number had grown to two in three reporters.

In terms of compatibility, Garrison found that some reporters were quicker to use the online resources than others. One reason was the lack of time to experiment with researching versus completing their usual daily tasks of covering the news.

> Some individuals were more venturesome and adopted early, others had higher thresholds or resistance to innovation and were more likely to adopt later. . . . Clearly, with any technology, there are risks in use and some adopters are reluctant to place themselves in vulnerable positions on deadline or at other times when completion of work is the highest priority. (Garrison, 2001, p. 233)

Research shows that Twitter has a similar effect. Given that reporters are constantly on deadline and tweeting out story updates is one more task that cuts into their time to report and write stories (Parmelee, 2013).

Frambach and Schillewaert (2002) concluded that innovations are not diffused unless the relevant individuals "buy into using them." This fits with Rogers's diffusion of innovation theory in that it shows the innovation, to be adopted, must be compatible with a person's life. Outside factors, such as training, personal innovation and experience with technology all contribute to motivating individuals. An innovation must appear as an advantage that is compatible with their existing routines. For example, if people see their peers and friends using the Internet for research, they may do the same as a way to keep up with their colleagues. That illustrates Rogers's test of observability – others will see the innovation in use.

Rogers' theory of diffusion of innovation provides a good framework for studying the use of Twitter in newspapers. For instance, his four components of diffusion are a good way to analyze how Twitter is viewed and used, how it is spread among colleagues, how long the process takes and the role of opinion leaders in that process.

Understanding newsrooms and the growth of Twitter

Twitter was invented in 2006 and immediately sparked interest among researchers who wanted to see how the new social media platform would change traditional journalism.

One theme of study is how Twitter enhances a more democratic journalism environment because it allows a once-passive audience to participate in what is discussed. (Shirky, 2008.) Poell and van Dijck (2014) studied how social media have affected news selection, production and dissemination of major media outlets, such as The New York Times and Los Angeles Times, as well as newer publications such as The Huffington Post. For instance, they found that metrics of what stories are most viewed by readers influence what gets the best play. In addition, this information is shared with advertising and marketing departments to target specific audiences for advertisers. The scholars, like a lot of professional journalists, believe such metrics-driven forces compromise journalistic independence. They also found that social media have an impact on how a newsroom operates. For instance, the media outlets place greater emphasis on reporters' blogging before the traditional practice of putting the most effort into a more complete newspaper story or broadcast.

Hedman (2015) did a survey of about 1,400 Swedish journalists to gauge how Twitter has been incorporated into their journalistic routines. A majority agreed that Twitter enhances discussions on news and offers tips or angles on stories. Seventy-six percent of daily tweeters agreed that the audience has gained more influence on media content in the past decade. The study's author suggests that the influence of Twitter may also reflect what Hermida (2013) describes as younger, multi-media savvy journalists being less constrained by older professional norms.

One of the changes caused by social media is how and when journalists distribute breaking news or scoops. Traditionally, newsrooms held back their biggest scoops for their own websites or print edition because they feared their competitors would find out about their exclusives. Now, social media mean breaking news has to be moved before it's old or leaked via various instant platforms. Witness the U.S. Airways plane crash on the Hudson River. A ferry passenger broke the news by tweeting the photo as he crossed the river. (Murthy, 2011.)

The same thing happened with breaking news of the raid on Osama Bin Laden's compound and the Boston Marathon bombings (Elliott, 2013.) Canter (2014) found that the order of newsgathering had changed with Twitter now ranking as the first place where journalists posts photos and blurbs about breaking news before posting them to the newspaper's website or writing for the print edition. This confirmed that journalists view Twitter as a mainstream publishing platform, not just another fad. Indeed, it allows smaller news organizations to compete along national and international news outlets to break news on a global platform.

Another change brought about from social media is using Twitter and Facebook to find story sources or tips. Canter (2014) found that journalists view Twitter as an invaluable newsgathering tool for getting information for stories or finding sources. But she did not find evidence to support Twitter changing the level of transparency or accountability among journalists. Nor did journalists use Twitter to test out story ideas with readers.

The role of journalist as gatekeeper remains intact, according to Canter (2014) findings, because there is even more information coming from around the globe via tweets. Journalists still verify that information before posting it to their own accounts or retweeting it.

One of the greatest barriers in the adoption of new technologies is getting all levels of players to share expectations about the usefulness of the new gadget or software and what will be measured or counted as a successful adoption of it. Managers are often given year-end bonuses based on revenue goals or profit margins.

Reporters and photographers are not part of that stratosphere, so they pay less attention to quarter-to-quarter results and just focus on what has to be done that day. So any adoption of technology must start with a shared vision, or it will fail. Orlikowski and Gash (1994) found that the adoption of new technologies is often stymied by senior management's failure to communicate their expectations for a new technology to the staff.

Most news organizations have their set goals, including producing high-quality journalism that will attract and retain readers, which, in turn, attracts advertisers who want those readers to see their ads, and, it is hoped, buy their products (Craft & Davis, 2013). Newsroom managers report to the owners, now largely one of six giant corporations such as News Corporation or Gannett, which demand a certain level of profitability so they can continue their operations, while satisfying shareholders with adequate per-share income and dividends (Bagdikian, 2004). Meanwhile, staffers, such as reporters, city editors and photographers, are paid to break news that is fair, accurate and engaging. Individuals are less concerned about the organization's bigger picture as they are focused on their own careers, especially in a time where the parent organizations have fired so many of their colleagues to save money (Weaver, et al, 2007). Both the organization and the individuals are under pressure to produce the paper as well as provide frequent updates on the website, with less time to focus on pet projects versus the daily grind (Beam, Weaver & Brownlee, 2009). With the advent of Craigslist and its free classified ads, newspapers have seen a chunk of their advertising revenue disappear. The recession has battered the real estate and retail advertising segments. And younger readers are shunning the print editions for multiple free websites for their news. All of this has put pressure on news organizations to reduce newsroom and marketing budgets (Kirchoff, 2009).

Newspapers have different structures, depending on their size, which is generally measured in its actual print circulation, page counts, revenue generated, and, in the more recent and relevant digital publishing sphere, number of visitors to their websites. Smaller newspapers, such as community papers, are often owned by families. They do not have to answer to shareholders, but they have more limited budgets and smaller staffs. Indeed, staffs are so limited that one person could be doing both news reporting and selling advertising and be "acutely concerned about economic survival and hence could be expected to emphasize advertising, circulation and operating profit" (Donohue, Olien & Tichenor, 1989).

At the other end of the spectrum are the larger, metropolitan newspapers, that focus on larger cities and the surrounding suburbs where many of their readers live.

Case Studies of Four Newspapers

To gauge the impact of Twitter at U.S. metropolitan newspapers, four metropolitan newspapers—the *Atlanta Journal-Constitution*, the *Dallas Morning News*, the *Denver Post* and the *Tampa Bay Times*—were selected for case studies of how reporters and editors use Twitter. These four newspapers were picked because they have designated social media editors. In addition, all four newspapers are the largest in their states of Georgia, Texas, Colorado and Florida. The *Atlanta Journal-Constitution* has a daily circulation of 640,000. The *Dallas Morning News* has a daily circulation of about 409,000. The *Denver Post* has a daily circulation of about 416,000, and the *Tampa Bay Times* has a daily circulation of 245,000. This provided access to larger groups of reporters and editors in various departments, which helps show who is most active on Twitter. In addition, picking these four offers geographic diversity.

Each newspaper has served its regions and readers with distinction, standing up for Civil Rights and other social issues, often losing readers and prompting protests against its stances. By doing so, each one has built strong ties to their communities. They have all shrunk in circulation and staffs, but have still survived tumultuous times of recession and other forces that have caused other U.S. dailies to fold. Among journalists, these four papers are considered tops for their investigative work and feature writing.

The *Atlanta Journal-Constitution* is now the largest newspaper in the Southeast. The *AJC* was born of the merger of two newspapers in 2001, a common phenomenon where morning and afternoon papers joined forces to save money. The *AJC* has a rich history of being an early advocate of the Civil Rights movement, including page-one essays, a rarity in newspapers, by Ralph McGill, its editor and publisher from the 1940s to the 1960s. He was awarded the Pulitzer Prize for his work in 1959 (Georgiaencyclopedia.org, 2013).

Beyond the serious coverage of social issues, the *AJC* has reflected the changing face of the South as it evolved from a backwater, farm country to home to new urban centers, such as Atlanta. Coverage of the changing landscape was captured from the 1970s through mid-1990s in the witty commentaries by Lewis Grizzard, who portrayed Southerners as "rednecks" with a mix of ridicule and respect. His columns were eventually syndicated to 450 newspapers and led to publication of 25 humor books, including "Elvis is Dead and I Don't Feel So Good Myself." Grizzard, who used a truck gun rack to hold his golf clubs, reflected what a lot of Southerners felt. For instance, he often reminded Northern transplants who complained about Southern ways that Delta airlines was on standby to fly them back North. Like the newspaper, Grizzard was trying to figure out the balance between the old Southern ways and the fast-moving expansion of Atlanta into a major economic hub (Cobb, 2013).

The *AJC* has developed a reputation of being innovative in digital platforms, especially during times of crisis. During the winter of 2014, snow and ice storms crippled Atlanta. During the storms, it was difficult to deliver the print edition, but the *AJC* beefed up its online presence, which accounted for more than 12 million page views across all platforms (NAA, 2014).

The *AJC* is owned by Cox Enterprises, a privately-held, $16-billion company controlled by heirs of James Cox, who started the empire by buying the Dayton newspaper in 1898. Cox became governor of Ohio and was defeated by Harding in his bid to become U.S. president (Coxenterprises.com, 2014). Cox also owns Cox Communications, a major player in the cable business, Manheim auto auctions and AutoTrader.com. The *AJC* has 150 employees in its newsroom, down from its peak of 500.

The *Dallas Morning-News* began publishing in 1885, when Alfred Belo wanted to start a sister publication for his *Galveston News*. The two were linked by correspondents feeding them news from around the state and were the first papers in the nation to publish simultaneous editions.

The paper pushed for improved municipal and health services and diversification of agriculture. In the early twentieth century, the News pushed progressive economic growth for the entire state of Texas. The newspaper established one of the country's first radio stations, WFAA, in 1922 (Vaugh, 2008).

Like the *AJC*, the *News* took a stand against racism when it condemned the Ku Klux Clan in the early 1920s. And it even stood up the state's booming oil business by refusing to accept any ads for oil stocks because it was nearly impossible to determine which ones were legitimate and which were frauds. Indeed, Adolph Ochs of the *New York Times* credited the *News* for helping to shape his "ideas and ideals" (Garrett & Hazel, 2010). The *News* enjoyed rapid growth, reaching a daily circulation of 525,000 in 2003. But the recession, loss of advertising and readers to the Internet has shrunk the circulation to 409,000. Its news staff has been halved from its peak of 600. It is still owned by the now-publicly traded Belo Corp.

The *Denver Post*, founded in 1892, has a colorful history starting with its owners, Harry Tammen and F. G. Bonfils. Competing against four rival daily newspapers, the *Post* became part of what one observed called "a three-ring circus." The *Post* resorted to printing headlines in red ink. After the death of Bonfils, his daughter revamped the *Post* and it became a more serious journalistic and dominant force in politics, becoming one of the first newspapers to condemn Sen. Joseph McCarthy's extreme tactics to investigate anyone suspected of being supportive of Communism.

The *Post* was eventually sold to Times Mirror, then MediaNews Group and is now owned by Digital First Media, which is controlled by a private equity, Aiden Global Capital (Hazlehurst, 2014). The newspaper has a strong reputation for public service reporting, such as its work in the mid-1980s on a series on missing children. It has been a leader in covering breaking news, such as the coverage of the Columbine High School shooting, the Aurora theater shooting as well as natural disasters of wildfires and mudsides. In total, the *Post* has won nine Pulitzer Prizes for such work.

One its current strengths is the cutting-edge approach to social media. Indeed, 27-year-old Dan Petty, who started as a *Post* intern, became the paper's first social media editor in April 2010. He is credited with helping to increase the *Post's* live video coverage, including a three-hour live show during the presidential debate at the University of Denver. Petty was named by *Editor & Publisher* as one of the "25 under 35" newspaper people to watch, which the publication said is proof that "newspapers are very much alive and kicking" (Yang & Zintel, 2014). The *Post* has 160 journalists in its newsroom.

The *Tampa Bay Times*, formerly the *St. Petersburg Times*, started as a weekly publication in 1884. The paper changed hands in 1912 when the Poynter family from Indiana purchased it with plans to expand during the boom times of the early 20th Century. The paper really flourished and grew to national stature under Nelson Poynter, who took over the paper from his father. Poynter, who did not like the encroachment of chains such as Knight-Ridder and Gannett, decided to leave ownership of his beloved *Times* to a media school, which was renamed the Poynter Institute after his death. New staff members are told the story about how Poynter's lawyer tried to dissuade him from shunning his heirs, to which the newsman replied: "I haven't met my grandchildren. I might not like them" (*Times* editors, personal communication, 1996).

Indeed, the *Times* enjoys a unique position among newspapers as the only thing resembling corporate headquarters is housed in one office now occupied by Paul Tash, who is both chairman of the Times Publishing Co. and the Poynter Institute. This is not an uptight corporate culture. Indeed, his predecessor, Andy Barnes, was lovingly called "Uncle Andy."

Unlike chain newspapers where editors are promoted from one city paper to bigger papers every few years, the *Times* has a tradition since the days of Nelson Poynter of grooming its leaders for years. There have been only three since Poynter died. Indeed, Tash likes to joke that he has had more wives than jobs—two wives, one job. He started as an intern and moved up the ranks of the city desk, Washington bureau, editor and now chairman.

The *Times* has a reputation for investigative journalism, such as its ongoing coverage of scientologists, which is headquartered in nearby Clearwater, Florida, and for ferreting out crooked politicians and sheriffs. The newspaper has won 12 Pulitzers, including one for inhumane treatment of homeless people in Tampa. The *Times'* newsroom has about 200 staffers.

These four newspapers represent what is still great about U.S. journalism—investigative and public service journalism, as well as a daily commitment to breaking news and telling readers what is going on. In addition, they represent what has gone on in the last 20 years, as newspapers try to remake themselves from daily print editions to a web and mobile world.

Instead of interviewing scores of reporters and editors at multiple newspapers, concentrating on four metropolitan newspapers provides a deeper understanding of the social systems, culture and practices in the newsrooms In addition, studying four metropolitan newspapers instead of the elite national media, such as the *New York Times* or the *Wall Street Journal*, offers a richer understanding of the broader U.S. newspaper industry's adoption of social media. The nation's largest newspapers have far greater resources of time, staff and money to devote to a more orchestrated social media campaign, as compared to the smaller, metropolitan newspapers, where individual reporters and departments are just now developing their strategies on how to best use social media.

This study shows how each has built its social media strategies during a time of great economic chaos. The 2008 collapse of the housing market and the recession that followed battered newspapers' advertising revenue from real estate and retail. In addition, Craigslist provides a free classified advertising, which was once a very lucrative category for newspapers. Indeed, print newspaper advertising dropped by 45 percent from $47.4 million in 2006 to $18.9 million in 2012 (Pew Research, 2013). Meanwhile, newspapers have seen their circulation numbers drop as more readers turn to the Internet for multiple choices for news. For instance, the *Tampa Bay Times* in the late 1990s had a daily circulation of over 300,000 copies. It has dropped to about 245,000 (*Tampa Bay Times* Media Kit, 2013).

The drops in revenue and circulation have been one driving force behind newspapers' efforts to improve their social media strategies. The spread of tablets and smart phones means newspapers need to figure out how new channels like Twitter can help them retain current readers and attract newer ones (Pew Research, 2013).

To learn about Twitter use and impact, fifty journalists at the four newspapers (and one volunteer from the Fort Worth Star-Telegram) were interviewed. The ages of the journalists—predominantly editors, reporters, online producers and editors—ranged from an average of thirty-one years old in Dallas to forty-five years old at the *Times*. The oldest respondents were 59 years old, while the youngest was a twenty-three-year-old crime reporter in Dallas. Three of the four newspapers—all but the *News*—have twenty-something-year-olds in specific social media leadership roles. The interviews were evenly divided between men and women.

Integrating Twitter into Changing Newsrooms

Given the pressures on newsrooms, editors are looking for ways to attract and retain readers who have more choices when it comes to picking a source for news. Specifically, scholars are looking at how social media platforms are being used in newsrooms.

According to journalists interviewed for this study, Twitter was not an immediate hit across newsrooms. Introduced in 2006, Twitter took a while to catch on with journalists. For some, the Green Movement, which challenged the Iranian government in the summer of 2009, was the point when they started to use Twitter to follow breaking news because information from official sources was so scarce. By late 2011, a Pew Research study of the Twitter feeds from 13 news outlets showed that use varied greatly: the *Washington Post* was tops, using 98 different organizational Twitter accounts, while the smallest organizations had just one and it was rarely used (Pew Research, 2011).

Tandoc (2013) studied three U.S. online newsrooms and surveyed editors to gauge how they were using both social media at web analytics to gauge the role of audience feedback. He found that journalists still relied on their imagined views of their audiences even when they have a lot of data from web analytics and social media. Indeed, the daily operations at the online news desk made decisions based on which stories generated the most reader clicks. Tandoc also found that audience feedback was used mainly to build on this and increase traffic to the newspaper's website. To a lesser extent, editors used Facebook and Twitter to interact with the audience. But it was mostly to seek comments, request photos or information for individual stories. In both his newsroom observations and survey of editors, Tandoc found that social media were used most often for promotion of content versus engagement with readers. He concluded that this use of technology involves a reworking of the individual journalist's role—journalists as marketer's of their own work, which blurs the traditional lines between the newsroom and business sides of media companies.

One of the biggest concerns about Twitter is the appropriate use of it in gathering the news when outsiders might not be as fair or accurate as professional journalists (Singer, 2010, Nieman Reports, 2012). In most professional news organizations, at least one or two editors read over reporters' copy for accuracy, fairness, and potential libel before publishing it. Citizens' contributions are often laced with opinions and lack accuracy checks. For instance, editors have no way of knowing if a video or photo has been altered. Singer (2010) found that legacy newsroom journalists' greatest concern about allowing outsiders to offer content is the "one-issue crackpots" trying to get their opinions into print. Hermida (2010) considers Twitter to be part of what he calls "ambient journalism" that is constantly on and updated, thanks to the explosion of cable television channels and the Internet. He agrees that professional journalists now face the challenge of deciding what on Twitter is useful information to be pursued and used, and what is just snark.

In one study, editors at the nation's largest newspapers said they do not use Twitter or other social media platforms for news content or to link to other sites other than their own (Ju, 2010). Smaller news organizations tend to welcome reader contributions, such as photos or feature items, as they have fewer staff reporters to create such lighter content (Ju, 2010). In some cases, newspapers such as *Le Monde* have allowed outside content, but preserve their gatekeeping role by posting it to a separate website, not the main news site (Singer, Hermida, et al., 2011).

Likewise, Lasorsa, Lewis and Holton (2012) studied how professional journalists navigate Twitter, in the context of professional norms and practices, by conducting a content analysis of more than 22,000 tweets from the journalists. They found that journalists more freely expressed their opinions, which contradicts the journalistic norm of impartiality and nonpartisanship. Twitter did allow journalists to be more transparent about how they do their work. The researchers noted that journalists working for the biggest, national publications were more likely to stick to traditional gatekeeping roles and to use Twitter as a one-way communication, not to link to other sites or to be chatty with readers. Holcomb, Gross & Mitchell (2011) findings were similar in showing that newsrooms are far less likely to use Twitter as a reporting tool or to recommend or curate other news organizations' work.

Given the proliferation of easy technology to transmit information, Twitter has aided the growth of "citizen journalism" where everyday people can build a website, blog or other content on whatever topic they find worthy of coverage. Researchers have studied whether Twitter has helped bridge the gap between legacy newsrooms and these amateur startups. Murthy (2011) studied whether Twitter signals a rise in citizen journalism or if it is a new means for mainstream media to find a scoop. The author found that the legacy media are much more open to using Twitter as a tip sheet on breaking news, such as the Mumbai bomb blasts or the crash of the US Airways jet into the Hudson River. The citizen journalists who post first are left unnoticed in most of the cases, however. Barnard (2012) did a case study of journalists' tweets to study how Twitter has helped new media platforms and citizen journalists. He concluded that Twitter has shifted the boundaries of the journalism field, integrating the values and practices of citizen journalists with those of professional journalists.

Researchers who have studied both the academic literature and professional practices of newsrooms have sought to compile the best practices that address both the journalists' and readers' interests. Herrara and Requejo (2012) studied the academic literature on Twitter and the Twitter practices of the New York Times, the Washington Post, National Public Radio and others to devise a list of 10 ways newsrooms should use Twitter. They found the best practices are: have a human voice, acknowledge content from others, link to those external sources, listen and talk to users, provide useful information in an appealing way, conduct surveys with users, promote your most relevant content in an attractive way, use hash tags in a useful way, add multimedia content, recognize unique content of other sites, and synchronize with them.

Boyle and Zuegner (2012) used diffusion of innovations theory to study Twitter use at 70 medium newspapers. The authors found that medium-sized newspapers tweeted about 82 times during one week of study, mostly during traditional business hours. Local news, which is a medium-sized newspaper's main focus, is the most tweeted topic. The authors found that relationship between the sizes of a newspaper, in terms of circulation numbers, and how much the staff tweets. In terms of diffusion of innovation, the authors found that two factors influence adoption of such innovations as Twitter—compatibility and complexity. Twitter is free and easy to learn, which means it faces less resistance than, say, introduction of a new publishing software.

Other studies have looked at adoption of Twitter and use as one more journalistic tool. Buttry (2011) did a popular press review of how most top U.S. newspaper editors shun Twitter. He argues that editors need to be active on Twitter because it's key to making the transition into the digital future. It shows a willingness to change. Editors "need to suffer the discomfort of learning publicly" how to take on this new technology. If editors do not embrace Twitter, the staff will follow that lead and be lazy, timid or arrogant about Twitter's potential as a news tool. Indeed, Dugan (2011) did a similar non-academic essay on how only three of the top 10 U.S. editors engage on Twitter. Only Bill Keller of the New York

Times, Kevin Convey of the New York Daily News and Gerould Kern of the Chicago Tribune were active on Twitter at the time of the study.

Another layer of analysis of Twitter's use as a journalistic tool considered how it was used in the coverage of specific events. Holcomb, Gross, and Mitchell (2011) conducted one of the broadest studies, analyzing more than 3,600 tweets from various news organizations' for one week. On average, newsrooms had forty-one different Twitter feeds. The Washington Post leads the pack with staffers posting to ninety-eight different Twitter accounts. Most newsroom tweets provided links back to the newspaper's website, which is key to driving online readership and advertising revenue. Greer and Yan (2010) did a content analysis of 141 community newspapers to see how Facebook, Twitter, and other social media tools are being used to deliver the news and connect with readers. They found that the smallest of community papers lagged the larger outlets in the adoption of social media tools. The same was true with medium-sized papers lagging the larger papers. One big issue facing all newsrooms is the lack of staff time required to constantly feed Twitter accounts. The smallest papers still face the digital divide because much of their readership is in remote areas and still lack high-speed Internet. Of the 141 newspapers studied, about 28 percent used Twitter. Sonderman and Beaujon (2013) analyzed a Twitter study of 150 journalists and news organizations' use of hashtags and URLs to increase engagement. They found that tweeting an event increases reader engagement by 50 percent. In addition, sharing others' content via links can build the overall conversation.

Scholars and journalists are finding that Twitter is increasingly influential in the coverage of politics. CNN journalist Peter Hamby (2013) interviewed more than seventy journalists and political strategists who worked on the 2012 presidential campaigns. Using Republican Nominee Mitt Romney's campaign as a case study, Hamby concluded that the instantaneous nature of social media now means any gaffe or stumble now becomes the story in hours, even minutes. He argues that Twitter is now the central news source for the Washington-based political press corps.

In other studies, scholars analyzed one major news event to see how Twitter was deployed in that coverage. Vis (2013) studied more than 700 tweets from Paul Lewis of The *Guardian* and Ravi Somalya of The New York Times during their coverage of the four-day riots in UK during the summer of 2011. The author coded the tweets to measure events such as reporters reporting first-hand accounts of news, quoting other news sources or retweeting reactions from citizens. The study showed extensive use of Twitter to share images as well as first-hand accounts of the riots.

Ahmad (2010) studied the London *Guardian's* use of Twitter in the protests of the G20 economic meetings in 2009. By using his firsthand observations of the newsroom's practices, in addition to a textual analysis of news and features, the researcher found that Twitter was a successful tool in live coverage of breaking news, allowing a newspaper to compete with television.

To understand the role of Twitter in the newsroom, some researchers have gone straight to readers to ask them why they follow news organizations' tweets. In the early days of Twitter, researchers found some reluctance to use it as serious news monitoring tool, largely because its earliest days were known for celebrity gossip and idle chitchat.

Arceneaux and Weiss (2010) also found that it also took some time to be embraced, just like many other technological breakthroughs. Recall that citizens were leery of the new technologies in the early days of the telegraph and the Internet, so it is normal that Twitter was met with some skepticism. But the amount of positive news coverage about Twitter has helped users warm to it and give it a try, according to their research.

For some news organizations, Twitter's primary purpose is promoting existing content in print or online publications, rather than as a surveillance tool for reporters. Blasingame (2011) studied Texas TV stations' use of Twitter and found that it was used primarily for promoting the stations' news content. Likewise, Ferguson and Greer (2011) studied how 111 radio stations were using Twitter by conducting a content analysis of the radio programs. The authors found that music stations used Twitter to promote the station, while the news stations tweeted more about actual news coverage, suggesting that the news stations are trying to cement their place as a news provider versus those that focus just on music. Messner, Linke and Eford (2011) studied the adoption and use of Twitter by newspapers and TV stations by doing a content analysis of the news organizations' tweets. The scholars found that news organizations are slow to use Twitter as a community-building tool. Instead, it's just one more promotional tool for existing content. Indeed, 25 percent of the news organizations studied did not put out a single tweet on the day of the analysis.

Armstrong and Gao (2010) studied promotion versus newsgathering in both broadcast and print newsrooms. The researchers found that broadcasting companies were more likely to use Twitter to promote their multimedia packages as compared to print newsrooms. In terms of what gets tweeted, they found that crime and public affairs stories were the most tweeted news content. Lifestyle content was the third most tweeted. Researchers noted that the sample period was May-August, a time when there is a lull in sports coverage, which could explain why this popular topic did not make the top three most tweeted stories. Interestingly, these findings contradict what the Project for Excellence in Journalism, which ranked the most popular tweets as: weather, national news, health, business and economy, international news, and science.

The bottom line for many news organizations is what tweeting does to increase traffic to their own websites, which can build advertising revenues because more page visits mean they can charge higher ad rates. But there is little evidence that tweets or other social media do much to move the needle. Ju (2010) analyzed the Facebook and Twitter use by 74 U.S. newspapers to evaluate the effectiveness of social network sites as news platforms. The author found no significant correlation between the number of social network subscribers and website visitors. The print editions proved to still be the greatest influence on driving traffic to the web site and social media. Hong (2012) analyzed the implications of newsrooms' adoption of social media and their online readership and how online traffic differs when using social media. The researchers found that social media generate less online traffic than search engines or news aggregators. The reason, they concluded, could be search engines have greater reach and spread information to broader audiences.

Understanding how Twitter is diffused throughout a newsroom is different from the earliest diffusion studies on farmers' adoption of new hybrid corn seeds. Farmers can see seasonal results in the quality of their corn harvest. Measuring the impact of Twitter use is more complicated because different people at different levels of newsrooms judge it through their own frames of reference.

TWO

Twitter Met with Great Skepticism

Twitter can represent a breakthrough in speedy communication. It can be embraced as an immediate headline service for news junkies. It can be a way to share jokes or pictures of nachos.

For this study, reporters and editors shared their experiences about the various stages of adoption and use of Twitter. Very few of the journalists interviewed had a positive opinion of Twitter when it first debuted. Instead, it was mocked as a place where people showed pictures of their dinners. But as journalists experiment with Twitter, they begin to get hooked once they see the benefits that the social media platform, such as expanding their list of sources and gathering information from distant places.

Twitter allows people to send out 140-character messages, often including a link to a news website, to alert the world of breaking news. The brevity of the content was one of the reasons that many of the journalists interviewed say they initially did not take it seriously, dismissing it as a source for fluff or celebrity gossip. The initial reception is reminiscent of when Gannett introduced *USA Today* in 1982. It offered brightly colored graphics and shorter, breezier news instead of the traditional gray pages and longer stories found in most newspapers. Veteran journalists chided it, calling it "McPaper" (Reuters, 2012).

Likewise, Twitter was greeted with a chorus of doubt in newsrooms. Chris Vognar, *Dallas Morning News* movie critic, recalls hearing about Twitter while on a Nieman fellowship at Harvard. "A lot of us thought it was funny and mocked it quite a bit" (C. Vognar, personal communication, April 23, 2014). Adds Dallas managing editor George Rodrique: "My first impression was what on earth can you say in 140 characters?" (G. Rodrique, personal communication, April 26, 2014). Craig Pittman, environmental reporter at the *Tampa Bay Times,* admits he was quite skep-

21

tical of Twitter in the early days. "I had this image of this is where people post pictures of their food," Pittman said. "We had an intern who asked me 'Do you have a Twitter account?' I told him: 'No, people would find my life boring'" (C. Pittman, personal communication, April 15, 2014).

But as each journalist tried Twitter, they started to see its potential as a tool in their work. When asked how they now define twitter to someone who had never heard of it or used it, the journalists had a wide range of definitions. Many compared it to other innovations, often dated to their own experiences, such as Bud Kennedy, a metro columnist at the *Fort Worth Star-Telegram*, who likened Twitter to a "modern day version of the CB radio," which was big in the 1970s, especially among truck drivers who wanted to know where the speed traps lurked or which diners offered 24-hour showers (B. Kennedy, personal communication, March 25, 2014).

Others define it as an index to world events that makes it easier to sort through the deluge of information sources. It is a compatible tool for their daily routines of constantly looking for news. "It's a table of contents of the world," said Joe DeLuca, publisher of the tampabay.com, the *Tampa Bay Times'* website. (J. DeLuca, personal communication, March 20, 2014). "It can't give you the depth of information that a piece of journalism can, but it can tell you 'this is out there.' This is something people are interested in right now." Michael Kruse, an enterprise reporter at the *Times*, has set up his Twitter feeds based on personal and professional interests, such as other Florida media outlets, magazines where he publishes freelance articles and news about his hometown of Boston. "I can see what I need to see more quickly and efficiently" (M. Kruse, personal communication, July 25, 2014).

Many of the journalists interviewed have shunned Facebook because they believe it is has become a dumping ground of useless information. "Twitter is a lot more concise and has a lot less crap," said Melissa Lyttle, a *Times* photographer (M. Lyttle, personal communication, July 25, 2014). She quit Facebook for a couple years because "I didn't like these people in high school and I don't want to see pictures of their kids. And how many OMG cat videos can I look at in one day?"

Journalists of all ages are engaging in Twitter, but many of the younger generation—those in the twenties and early thirties—view themselves as on the cutting edge of Twitter. The early adopters were "younger people like me," said Amber McDonald, the twenty-nine-year-old digital audience specialist at the *Times* (A. McDonald, personal communication, March 24, 2014).

"It's much more natural for my generation. My parents are a lot more active on Facebook," said Sarah Mervosh, a twenty-three-year-old criminal justice reporter in Dallas (S. Mervosh, personal communication, April 24, 2014). One reason is likely the prevalence of smart phones and easier mobile access to the Internet. That has been a given for younger reporters as compared to older reporters who were more tethered to their desktop computers and landlines. DeLuca at the *Times* describes smart phones as "an appendage" for millennials.

Katie Leslie, city hall reporter at the *AJC* said she is glad that she was on the leading edge of using Twitter in her work. "This is an older newsroom and some people see it as another thing I have to do. I get that. I feel that way about a lot of things. I saw value in it" (K. Leslie, personal communication, May 20, 2014).

Charles Gay, deputy managing editor for local news at the *AJC,* believes some of the veteran journalists are "intimidated" by new technologies, such as Twitter. "It's a newsroom. There are a certain number of hide-bound people. It's a culture we're trying to break" (C. Gay, personal communication, May 20, 2014). One reason some journalists are uncomfortable with Twitter is simply one more thing to do in their already busy days. "When I first started, we wrote stories and made photo assignments. That was it," Gay said. Twitter is "an added responsibility." Journalists are now expected to "become your own marketing department. You want your friends, followers, and people in the community to know what you're doing."

AJC reporter Leslie has seen that slowly change as more younger reporters have been added to the staff and Twitter has also become "a newsroom expectation," To be sure, there are exceptions. Bob Trigaux, a 59-year-old business columnist at the *Times,* was one of the first in that newsroom to use Twitter. He believes the *Times* could do a better job encouraging all online activity more aggressively, ranging from always filing a story online first and fast, to being more aggressive on Twitter. "It still feels early on in our efforts," he said (B. Trigaux, personal communication, March 27, 2014).

Clearly, that sense of urgency in adopting new technologies such as Twitter starts with the individuals, regardless of their age. But it can be fostered to a greater extent when journalists see those in their peer group embracing it. Based on the interviews, there were no signs that Twitter adoption and use differs between men and women journalists. The only exception appears to be in sports coverage because those beats are still covered predominantly by men in these four newsrooms. But in other subject teams, beats are covered equally by both men and women. To be sure, men dominate senior management at all four newspapers.

Editors do have a different approach to Twitter as many of the most senior editors clearly want reporters to take the lead on feeding social media from the front lines, concentrating instead on using their Twitter accounts to promote the papers' work, shilling for their marketing departments or just shooting the breeze about sports. Consider tweets on the randomly picked days of July 8 to 11 by the top editors at the four newspapers. Kevin Riley, editor at the *AJC* and Gregory Moore at the *Post* tweeted about the big sports news. "I have LeBron fever. . . . Exiting moment for Cleveland. Good luck," Moore tweeted. Neil Brown, editor of the *Times*, tweeted that the *Times* won the contract to distribute *USA Today* on the Gulf Coast. *News* editor Bob Mong tweeted the most news during that time, with updates on the city of Dallas' plans to add light rail to the airport. On June 26, 2014, Riley tweeted about the Georgia Supreme Court, Mong tweeted about the *News'* winning four feature awards, Moore retweeted a *New York Times* feature about the only first round NBA pick who never played for the leagues and Brown at the *Times* did not tweet that day.

The feedback from reporters and editors shows how a new innovation such as Twitter spreads inside an organization, overcoming hurdles such as being mocked as a toy for Hollywood celebrities.

TWITTER: A TECHNOLOGICAL EXTENSION TO REPORTING

In an era of downsized newspaper staffs, Twitter has been embraced as an innovation that helps journalists attain one of their top goals—being first with the news. Middle management editors vary in their usage, depending on their roles. But features editors tend to shun Twitter. Amanda Wilkins, senior digital editor for entertainment and lifestyles at the *News*, shared her opinion: "Honestly, I don't tweet a lot. I think it's the copy editor mentality . . . being behind the scene is okay with me." She does use Twitter to interact with employees and she has embraced it as a marketing tool to promote the paper's content (A. Wilkins, personal communications, April 24, 2014).

News breaking news editor Matt Peterson considers it invaluable in his role as editor of general assignment reporters and interns. "It's the first program I fire up in the morning to see what happened overnight. To keep up with the competition, you need to be Twitter literate. That's where everyone is putting their stuff first" (M. Peterson, personal communication, April 24, 2014). Indeed, Peterson sees Twitter as a technology that has changed the entire mindset of newspapers. Before Twitter, "we were more interested in getting (the whole story). Accuracy is still the first thing, but we're very much interested in getting it first."

Leslie, the *AJC's* city hall reporter, puts it bluntly: "If you don't have it on Twitter first, you didn't have it first." She now writes a short website story only after she has sent out a few tweets of breaking news.

Twitter is especially helpful in following up on tips from an overnight freelance reporter who monitors the police scanners. The Dallas police department now has several patrol officers sending out tweets from crime scenes. "The police chief is not the most media friendly guy so I think this is almost a way to be in competition with the newspaper," Peterson said. "It's to control their message and show they are in tune with the community and show they are real people, too." Regardless of the police department's motives, the blogs and tweets can lead to getting photos from crime scenes.

Likewise, it helps Peterson's team move quickly from rumor to fact when news is breaking. He recalled when tornadoes struck a Texas school:

> Nobody knew anything. We didn't have reporters right there at the time. The emergency management people will not give you anything until they're at the scene. We put the name of the elementary school into the tweet deck and immediately we were seeing things from parents saying the kids are fine. You get to a critical mass (of information) and you feel confident to report yes, some damage to the school, but no injuries. People want to know that as soon as possible. Without Twitter, we would've had to wait for hours before we learned something.

Twitter is also embraced as a new technology to locate people who can contribute to their coverage of their beats. For instance, Twitter is said to be a fast way to find sources, especially when news is breaking. Instead of the old-fashioned reporting methods of going door-to-door or telephoning people, Twitter allows journalists to post a question and reach people around the globe. The *Denver Post* business staff was covering the General Motors' recall of autos with faulty ignition switches. Given the age of the cars, they faced difficulties finding owners of the vehicles, so they tweeted out a request for owners to contact the paper.

They found a Colorado man who owned one of the cars, but he was working at a research station in the South Pole. So the reporter interviewed him via Twitter. "It gets us to people we couldn't get to," said Dana Coffield, the *Post's* business editor (D. Coffield, personal communication, May 28, 2014).

Reporters note that Twitter is popular with younger sources, who use it as their main medium for communicating with their friends. *Dallas Morning News* education reporter Tawnell Hobbs uses Twitter to find students and teachers for sources in stories. She recalled one story about a teacher who had posed for *Playboy*, which prompted the district to fire her.

Hobbs got on Twitter and found "the kids were already talking about this. They always hit you back." This helped fill in the context of the story because the teacher and the school district declined to talk to the media. "On Twitter, she said 'sorry kids. I got fired today,' " Hobbs said. Twitter has helped her track down friends and family when students get killed (T. Hobbs, personal communication, April 23, 2014)."If you put the kid's name in the search bar, you see tweets of condolences. They are on there and they lay out their emotions and tell you what's going on," Hobbs said. She has a student directory, which includes home phone numbers, but it has not proved as valuable as Twitter. "These kids for some reason want to communicate electronically. First place they are going is Twitter."

Just as Twitter is a hangout for teens, it has also been embraced as a "cool" toy for sports junkies. Editors and reporters at all four newspapers agreed that sports coverage is a natural for Twitter largely because of the play-by-play nature of football or baseball as well as the religious-like following by fans. "In digital, it is massive. It's the intensity of the audience," *AJC* managing editor Bert Roughton said (B. Roughton, personal communication, May 20, 2014). Mobile devices "are toys. It's boys playing with toys." Other research has shown the rise of multiple screen use by young men, especially during sporting events. They like the camaraderie of tweeting with friends, reading others tweets, while watching the game on television.

David O'Brien, who covers the Atlanta Braves baseball team, is one of the paper's most popular writers on Twitter. He tweets the entire game so it's a "cool way for people to see the story build." Roughton has considered reprinting the Twitter stream in the print edition. "It's not a bad narrative."

TWITTER BUILDS NEW CONVERSATIONS

For some journalists, Twitter is embraced as an innovation because it is a new avenue to build more connections with readers who are familiar with their work and people who have never picked up the newspaper. Matthew Haag, one of the education reporters at the *Dallas Morning News*, views this practice as an extension of how newspapers generated conversations among people.

> Years ago, people would get the paper and open it on the breakfast table and it was part of the conversation. The conversation now is happening on Twitter and Facebook. It is imperative to be a part of those conversations. Twitter is a medium that people have embraced. If you're not part of it, you're missing out on so much. You're missing out on the conversation about news and what's happening in our world. We're even more connected as people. We're meeting those people online and getting their perspective. It's having a conversation about what's happening, just with more people. (Personal communication, M. Haag, April 25, 2014)

This becomes increasingly important to reporters like Haag because they are receiving fewer emails from readers. "I don't know if it's the decline in circulation or the advent of comments on stories. (Readers) feel less of a need to talk to us," Haag said. He considers the Twitter conversations to be more "candid and personal exchanges." It keeps journalists more accountable. Another advantage: His Twitter page lists his phone numbers, which readers have used to pass along tips or feedback on his work.

Using Twitter to build connections with the community illustrates the literature on building social capital. If journalists feel more invested because of Twitter exchanges, that strengthens their bonds with readers. Social capital is made up of social obligations or connections (Bourdieu, 1986). Social capital is what a person gains by participating in a community, whether geographically-located such as a church or virtually situated such as Facebook. Bourdieu (1986) said the amount of social capital one person gains is dependent on the number of people in the overall network. The size of that bigger group is a result of how much time the individual invests in establishing or reinforcing ties with others. As this capital builds, it is accessible to all who help accrue it.

Putnam (2000) argued that the decline of two-parent households, dwindling membership in churches or bowling leagues and the rise of television and the Internet have eroded social capital in the United States. But other scholars have found that the Internet has actually increased social capital through social networking sites such as Facebook and Twitter. These global Internet sites give participants loose ties to larger networks of people, which give them access to more resources than what they find within the confines of their geographic communities (Donath & Boyd, 2004).

Researchers have noted the importance of Internet-based relationships to strengthen ties with others. One reason is technology enables users to share interests and access to distribution lists, directories or search capabilities that can help them continue to broaden their ties with outsiders. As users tap into these technologies, they build and maintain an even bigger network of relationship that provide additional resources. Ellison, Steinfield, and Lampe (2007) sought to explain technology's impact on social capital in their research on Facebook and college students. They found a positive relationship between Facebook use and the maintenance and creation of social capital. One reason is Facebook is easy to use. Even those who are shy can initiate a conversation or respond to others online.

Those who were initially turned off by the deluge of information and tweets from people they do not know came to appreciate it as broadening their network.

"The thing that made me skeptical in the beginning is what I love now," says *Dallas Morning News* political editor Ryan Rusak (R. Rusak, personal communication, March 24, 2014). "We're connecting with people [we] don't know." He uses Twitter to follow what his competitors are writing and to find "good things to read, both professionally and personally. It's a really good clip service," he said. "You can have actual conversations with readers and learn what they want to know," Rusak said.

When the *Star-Telegram's* Kennedy went to the Democratic National Convention, journalists were encouraged to use Twitter to get notifications about protests, street blockages, marches and other logistics affecting the convention. He initially used it to tweet a few things from the convention floor, then he posted his stories. Now, he follows a set schedule of tweeting out his columns around 9 a.m., then posts some other news tidbit around lunch and again at 4 p.m.

> I make it a news bulletin service. I see it as an extension of my column. I have two rules for my column: I go out every day and tell readers every thing I find out. I write everything I know. But I also make it broad and include links to good stories from other newspapers. My goal is to make it one feed about everything going on in Fort Worth."

Kruse, the enterprise reporter at the *Times,* believes Twitter allows him to "provide a service to my followers."

> They know I read the *New York Times* and the *Tampa Bay Times* pretty early and that I'm going to tweet stories, thoughts, stats or items of interest from those reading rhythms. They have come to expect that more toward evening, they will get a by-product of my night time reading, which is more magazine heavy. Throughout the day, I tweet things that are in the air right now…I think that's why they're following me. I sort of have this unwritten formula in my head that says "you're going to be very self-promotional at some point. I earned the right to send out those links if I did shared a bunch of other stuff as well."

Some journalists have used the Twitter conversations as a training tool. Lyttle, the *Times* photographer, mentors the newspapers' interns and has used Twitter to send out darts and laurels without naming names. "They do something universally dumb that people can learn from," she said. She used #tbtintern to tweet about the *Times* selection process of the photography interns. She had to whittle down 100 applicant portfolios to a more manageable pool for the photo editor. As she found strengths and weaknesses, she tweeted about what makes a good photo. The tweets were so popular that a University of Georgia professor shared them as part of his teaching. Other photographers tweeted asking her to critique their work because "no one been brutally honest with them." The photo editor at *Time* magazine tweeted to aspiring photographers looking for work: "Follow Melissa Lyttle for great advice and laughs."

Talking with reporters and editors showed a remarkable amount of agreement about the benefits of Twitter, even across the four different newsrooms. What started as a strange novelty has been embraced as a technological innovation that gives journalists quick access to information and people around the globe. It has helped newsrooms be more nimble about getting news out to readers and injected a greater sense of urgency to be first on Twitter, not on the paper's website, as the social media platform has a far greater reach. This makes journalists happy because their goal is to get the news out to as many people as possible.

As a news-gathering tool, Twitter can be a tip sheet and quick summary of what's going on in the world and on topics they cover. They can follow their competitors and see what they are writing. The interviews illustrate one of the requirements of Rogers' diffusion of innovation theory—a new technology must provide a visible improvement over the past before it's adopted as an every day tool. And Twitter enriches the conversations between readers and reporters, a relationship that has often been strained because the old letters to the editor or phone calls were generally ignored by journalists. "You can't have coffee with everyone who reads your stuff and you don't want to because half of them are crazy," said Sarah Blaskovich, digital entertainment editor at the News (S. Blaskovich, personal communication, April 24, 2014). "Twitter is a way to talk to so many more people."

It is clear that Twitter has deepened the relationship that journalists have with their audience, which enhances the social capital of both the reporters and the news organization. Reporters go beyond sharing their own links; they act as an information distillery of work they've read elsewhere as a way to enrich their readers' lives. In the process, they often find new story ideas and sources—sometimes even in the South Pole.

THREE

The Importance of Family and Friends

Rogers's diffusion of innovation theory suggests that innovations must be advantageous as well as (1) talked about (2) proved easy to use (3) considered an improvement over the past before they have a chance to spread inside an organization. In addition, (4) the spreading of the innovation depends on individuals being willing to trust their colleagues' opinions of the new technology and train one another. Thus, social capital theory relates to diffusion of innovation theory because adopting a new innovation like Twitter depends on the social system and its leaders. Opinion leaders and peers influence others in the social system of the newsroom. If individuals adopt Twitter, they boost their own social capital and improve their standing in the larger community of the newsroom.

Through the interviews, journalists said the adoption of Twitter is influenced both by technology leaders within newsrooms and by casual conversations with friends and family members. In some cases, reporters had to be told to try social media by their editors. Mostly, however, reporters and editors got hooked on Twitter as part of keeping up with their peers. Many journalists cited friendly rivalries with their colleagues as each tries to attract more followers than the other. In the world of Twitter, a person's number of followers is the mark of success on the social media platform.

COMMUNICATIONS CHANNELS AND KNOWLEDGE TRANSFER

At the *News*, journalists are told that using Twitter or other social media platforms must be part of their daily duties. "The buy-in has taken a long time," said Christy Robinson, digital community specialist at the *News*. She blames the "irascibility" of journalists. "They feel like they didn't get into journalism to do this thing that's marketing . . . I have friends who are personally shy who can't get past it as self promotion." In the case of some women journalists, Robinson said the paper has a "handful" who are "still afraid to do it because they do not want their picture posted on Twitter."

> It puts them out there and that worries them. But they are in harm's way already. I don't have a lot of sympathy for them. If they can't take the heat, they need to get out. Social media is part of the job. If some-body wants to kill you, they will kill you. And it's not just because they found you on Twitter. They can find you through your byline. (C. Robinson, personal communication March 26, 2014)

Robinson is particularly blunt about her belief that journalists are being overly dramatic about the dangers of being on Twitter. She was the only person interviewed who mentioned this reason for journalists' reluctance to use social media. More often, it was the stubbornness or curmudgeon-ly ways of reporters that kept them from experimenting with Twitter.

By far, most journalists said they adopted Twitter because of influence from peers, family, or friends. This is especially true when certain jour-nalists are seen as technology leaders in their news organizations. Jour-nalists have been asked to try a lot of new publishing systems over the years, so some can be reluctant to adopt yet another tool. At the *Tampa Bay Times,* that person was Matt Waite, one of the journalists who helped launch one of the *Times'* most successful online ventures, PolitiFact, a website that fact-checks claims made by politicians. He showed his friend and colleague Pittman the benefits of Twitter, which was enough for the environmental reporter to set up his own Twitter account. "I tend to follow the tech cues of Matt. I let Matt do the Beta test."

Kennedy, metro columnist at the *Star Telegram,* said he joined Twitter in 2008 for two reasons: peer and family pressure. "My friends told me I needed to get involved with social media in 2008. And my nephew in high school in Austin told me to get on Twitter."

Kevin G. Riley, editor of the *AJC,* got on Twitter in early 2009 after meeting with the newsroom bloggers. "They pressured me to get on Twitter and begin tweeting as the editor. They made a bunch of sugges-tions on what I should do. If you're not participating in it, it's hard to lead a newsroom that has to participate in it," Riley said. His greatest concern was putting himself out there for "relentless attacks" by fringe elements. "As the editor, you tend to hear from really hostile people on the fringe of issues." He gets some of that, but more often, he believes tweeting con-nects him with the audience. Sometimes in amusing ways: a diner recog-nized him at a local café and tweeted out that the *AJC* editor was eating breakfast. He also uses social media to engage readers in topics he's mulling for his twice-monthly column (K. Riley, personal communica-tion, June 18, 2014).

Gregory L. Moore, editor of the *Denver Post*, joined Twitter in 2010 while on vacation. Initially, he used it to tweet out his staff's work. Now he has expanded that to include interesting articles from other publications because "I connect them with things they don't know about."

He has realized that his staff watches closely what he tweets and they react. For instance, if he retweets something about TV commentator Howard Kurtz, his television writer will quickly respond that he already had that item in his blog and "can I get some love?" "They put so much time in (on their work) and it doesn't always hit the home page so I'm not aware of it," Moore said (G. Moore, personal communication, May 28, 2014).

The interviews showed that the most important communication channel in the adoption of Twitter in newsrooms is the influence of colleagues. Word spreads as journalists saw how it can help them find sources or get their stories out to a broader audience.

It is interesting to note that reporters were the trailblazers in all four of the newsrooms, not their bosses. And the senior editors have not been nearly as active as their staffs since then. For instance, Bob Mong, editor of the *News*, joined in August, 2011, and had tweeted about 1,800 times (as of July, 2014). Neil Brown, editor of the *Times*, joined in March, 2009, but has tweeted only about 200 times. To give some perspective, the *AJC*'s Braves reporter, David O'Brien, has tweeted 82,000 times since joining in October, 2009. This supports research by Dugan (2011) who found that only three of the top 10 U.S. editors engage on Twitter. Many of the editors said they view their roles as encouraging those on the front lines of news to use it, or they use it to promote the good work of their staffs.

EXPERIENCING TWITTER: COMPATIBILITY AND COMPLEXITY

One of the issues that determines whether someone adopts a new technology is whether it is easily tried or tested (Rogers, 1962). For journalists, adoption of Twitter requires they navigate the line between their personal and professional lives. For instance, journalists have to be careful what they write, even in their personal tweets, because the public always views them as representing a large news organization. Opinions expressed on Twitter can jeopardize their own and the newspaper's credibility with readers. Those who were early adopters often blended their own activities, such as pictures of their entrees when dining out with friends, with their tweets from work, such as sending out links to their latest stories.

That gave senior management at the Tampa Bay *Times* reason to move slowly in the adoption of the social media platform because they did not want any journalists' personal activities to sully the reputation of the *Times*' brand. "People following a reporter all of a sudden would see a tweet about a girl he just saw at McDonald's," said DeLuca, publisher of the website. "That was a real problem and from a leadership standpoint, that was what held (our adoption of Twitter) back."

Others have learned to not mix their professional Twitter account with their personal lives. One male reporter said this was a lesson they learned when they became passionate about their sports teams.

> I was watching a baseball game and the pitcher for the Rangers was in the 9th inning and it was a perfect game. He gave up a hit. I used the "F" word multiple times. I heard from a boss the next day. It wasn't a finger-wagging. It was more of a "gentle hand on the shoulder" and a reminder of "that probably wasn't the best idea." He handled it very well.

Another measure of Rogers' (1962) diffusion of innovations theory is whether the innovation is compatible with users' existing lifestyles, work patterns, and routines. Given that Twitter is a free service based on the Internet, Twitter appears to be quite compatible with journalists' routines. In addition, most of those interviewed said they use it while out of the office via their smart phones. And it is the first thing they check when they wake up in the morning, even before they get to their desks.

They also note that Twitter is often more compatible with the routines of their sources. Just as reporters use their mobile phones to constantly be in touch, busy sources find it easier to manage their conversations by using Twitter at their convenience.

Rusak, political editor at the *News*, views Twitter as sometimes less intrusive than calling because people can answer a tweet while in a meeting or doing other tasks versus having to stop everything and answer a ringing phone. "I reach out on Twitter versus cold calling or email and they are more likely to respond because there's a lower threshold there," Rusak said. Blaskovich, digital entertainment and music editor at the *News*, uses it to get to people who are "not answering their phones. Talking on the phone is tougher and tougher each year. They prefer to text or email me." This strategy worked when she was tracking down a local disc jockey who had been fired by a radio station. "He works weird hours. I sent him a direct message on Twitter while he was probably still in bed. He tweeted me back and said 'I'm up and moving at 11. You can call me on my cellphone.'"

Unlike calling a source for an interview, Twitter allows reporters to collect information a little at a time. For instance, Kennedy in Fort Worth, uses Twitter's direct messaging feature to conduct interviews, one tweet at a time. "It's quick, easy and I can do it without leaving my desk. You can have a conversation with someone without dropping what you're doing. And that person doesn't have to drop everything. By the end of the day, the interview is done."

CHANGING THE CULTURE AND ORGANIZATIONAL STRUCTURE TO INCORPORATE TWITTER

The *Times* formed a social media advisory group in 2013 to come up with guidelines and strategies on how to maximize the benefit of being on social media platforms. DeLuca and others gathered a team from various departments and named McDonald, digital audience specialist, as its chair. "We wanted to tap into the whole generation who use social media as an appendage. They understand it. I'm not of that generation…We're really listening to them…they are fabulously smart and creative."

The overall goal at the *Times* was to establish a social media presence that would cement the brand name, not dilute it with "17 different Facebook pages that look like 17 different companies," DeLuca said.

Another complexity of Twitter is figuring out the right blend of what and when to tweet. At the *News*, for instance, the social media team schedules tweets from sports and entertainment to go out at assigned times during the day. "There is a lot of competition internally to get on the flagship Twitter account," Wilkins said. "We had trouble getting things out." Her argument for more entertainment and lifestyle tweets is: "Can we give people something a little less doom and gloom?" Finding that right mix of hard news and lighter fare, along with how to have regularly scheduled tweets and still maintain some spontaneity and breaking news, is a challenge for all four newsrooms. Every department has its own ideas on what is the most important Twitter offering and what should go out on the flagship Twitter account versus individual reporters' tweets. "I'm not sure how much journalism world understands the value. We're still trying to figure it out. It's like the Baptist church. You have three lunches and 17 meetings before you do anything," Wilkins said.

Others argue that breaking news can get drowned out because of those scheduled tweets. "There's a disconnect on how Twitter is run," Mervosh said. "There will be breaking news, but we're still tweeting things about ice cream sundaes and puppies." She recalls when the fertilizer plant in West, TX exploded in April, 2013, killing 15 people and injuring more than 300. She describes the push to get the explosion news out on Twitter as having to "highjack the Twitter account for live tweeting."

Michael Landauer, digital communities manager at the *News*, supervises the social media team that runs the flagship brand's Twitter account. "In news, everybody wants to be tweeted on the house account," in addition to their own department or personal accounts, he said.

Another issue is balancing journalists' interest in following a lot of other people and organizations with the deluge of tweets that comes with following hundreds of others. "Twitter has been a victim of its own success," said one journalist, who asked to remain anonymous. "It has huge potential, but we could really spoil it for people because so many people are dumping so much stuff" (Anonymous, personal communication, 2014).

The sheer quantity of tweets impacts journalists' role as agenda setters in the news. Everyone can now reach journalists, so news organizations have the additional hurdle of sifting through the deluge to decide what gets priority on that day's agenda.

Getting a news staff engaged in a new technology also depends on working the new practice into the culture and professional norms already established. With Twitter, editors at the four newspapers are struggling with the balance between mandating that reporters hit certain quotas for social media participation versus trusting them to incorporate it into their daily routines.

Inside the *News*, there is considerable confusion about management's expectations for Twitter. Editors met with individuals and teams to establish individual goals on social media usage. Reporters were told to get comfortable with Twitter, Facebook, or other platforms and integrate regular postings into their workdays. This became part of their annual review, with social media quotas established for each person. But how that is interpreted and enforced is a source of dispute. One journalist, who asked to remain anonymous, is quite blunt about the subject:

> Do we have a clue what we're doing? We are making it up as we're going along. We've not received a lot of direction on what to do. There is a social media quota. What that led to is the department head to say to reporters. "How many did you write? About the same as last month?" That's junk. Measuring quality is much harder than measuring quantity. That's manufactured engagement. There are people who are really, really into it. Others who have no interest at all and are allowed to go on that way. (Anonymous, personal communication, 2014)

Another journalist, who asked to remain anonymous, said the guidance changes. For instance, staffers asked their bosses if it was okay to tweet that "George Bush is a nice man, but I don't agree with how he's running the country." They were told that was okay, as long as they didn't cover politics. "About six months ago, the same question was asked and we were told that's a firing offense" (Anonymous, personal communication, 2014).

The sentiments expressed by some journalists shows ambiguity, which Singer (2004) found when studying the convergence efforts at four U.S. newspapers. If management does not give clear directions, mandates will be ignored or be poorly enforced.

Dallas managing editor Rodrique said the social media quotas were met with skepticism. "Half of them thought it was an annoyance," he said. As for policies on tweeting, he describes the policy as "Do it, but do it wisely."

The *AJC* does not enforce a quota for social media engagement by their staff. Instead, editors want the staff to be active and use social media platforms to "tell stories, gather information, and share stories they are working on," said Monica Richardson, managing editor for digital and local news. The staffers who are most active on social media "tend to be our top performing reporters. They are engaged with followers and sources." (M. Richardson, personal communication, May 19, 2014).

At the *Times,* it is "important that (reporters) be on Twitter," but there is not a "hard and fast threshold. But it is important that everyone know how to use it," said McDonald, *Times'* digital audience specialist.

At the *Post,* there is no formal policy on how much the staff uses social media. "We recognize the value of the tool. We have to be a player. We know what it can do to extend the brand throughout the world. We don't have to do a lot of convincing," said Moore, *Post* editor.

Twitter also forces newspapers to confront a new source of news that is not always accurate. Traditionally, each reporter gathers facts from trusted sources and documents. With Twitter, anyone with a smart phone can now be a publisher, creating a flurry of bad information mixed in with legitimate, accurate news. That's a culture shift. It also reflects a change in traditional agenda-setting role of journalists.

News organizations tend to want to create their own content and not rely on untrained amateurs to contribute to their dispatches. Even professional news organizations get duped. For instance, both Fox News and NBC News incorrectly tweeted the death of Florida's longest serving congressman Bill Young in October, 2013. The mistake appears to have originated on Twitter with a Florida blogger named Peter Schorsch, who tweeted that the congressman had died, attributing the information to a member of the Young family, according to bustle.com.

And the professional journalists can also make bad calls on what to tweet. Rodrique said the newsroom has seen some "social media food fights. Even things that aren't brain surgery can be surprisingly difficult." When asked for examples, he replied: "That's something we don't want to talk about. People are people especially in the heat of a give and take and they say things they regret."

The *News* was criticized after the sports department tweeted about a photo slideshow created to introduce readers to the new University of Texas coach Charlie Strong. Legendary football coach Lou Holtz once described Strong as "not a hip hop coach." The tweet went out without attributing the quote to Holtz, leading readers to believe this was a commentary from the *News,* not Holtz's opinion. "It looked mildly racist, maybe pretty racist, so a lot of people pounced on it," Landauer said. "It was not our best moment. One of the lessons there was it doesn't take much to start a little fire."

The *AJC* took some heat for this tweet: "$1M Lottery winner Willie Lynch can get 40 acres and a whole lotta mules." The tweet was considered racist by many readers because it made light of what General William Tecumseh Sherman promised to freed slaves after the end of the Civil War. In addition, others on Twitter pointed out that the African American lottery winner has the same name as a slave owner who allegedly counseled other plantation owners on how to control their slaves. The *AJC* removed the tweet and issued an apology.

It was a blow to the *AJC*, which has a solid place in history as an early and staunch defender of civil rights. "We're in the South," Gay said. The AJC is "still considered a big institution that has not always cared about what's happening. It was a set back." While media commentators speculated that someone would be fired for the tweet, no one lost their job because of the incident. Editor Riley held a staff meeting at which he tried to reassure nervous staffers who were now hesitant to use Twitter. Riley told the staff to "continue to be out there on Twitter and use good judgment," said reporter Scott Trubey. "This paper has built up a reputation of a century of good journalism. Having your boss go out there and say he still wants you to be out there on Twitter and engage in it and be entertaining and informative was a big relief" (S. Trubey, personal communication, May 20, 2014).

Riley said the staff had additional training on social media after the event. "The reality is we are still depending on the judgment and the dedication of our journalists. We need to always remember that," Riley said.

Editors are reluctant to talk about personnel issues or punishment handed out for missteps on social media. Based on what editors said in interviews, no one has been fired solely for their comments on social media. Instead, mishaps have led to more training and meetings to remind people to avoid delicate subjects such as race or sex.

PEER AND EXPERT OPINIONS ABOUT TWEETING

The final element influencing adoption of Twitter is whether the technology is observable to others. In the case of Twitter, do journalists' peers, bosses, and readers notice it?

The *Times'* business columnist Trigaux, a veteran of 35 years as a business journalist, saw how much his tweeting got noticed in his 2013 coverage of Progress Energy's failed Crystal River nuclear power plant. Duke Energy bought out Progress Energy and inherited the nuclear plant in the deal and determined it was not worth the price of fixing it. Instead, Florida's Public Service Commission, which oversees rates charged by utility companies, allowed Duke to pass along the cost of decommissioning the plant on to consumers through higher utility bills.

> There was a growing revolt by readers. When this particular story came out about the PSC abdicating to Duke and penalizing rate payers, this was a particularly boisterous column. It got a lot of feedback and it played fairly heavily on Twitter. That is one that generated a lot of hits to the link with additional responses and emails. All were expressions of outrage.

Twitter is viewed as an innovation because retweeting a colleague's story is embraced as a virtual pat on the back. This appears to be increasingly important as news staffs continue to shrink as corporate owners impose budget cuts and layoffs to build profits. The cuts have been deep and painful at the *News*, where the news staff has shrunk from 600 to 260 people. "The newsroom doesn't have the bodies," said Robert Wilonsky, digital managing editor. "We all carry more buckets." Wilonsky writes as a "stop-gap measure" to get the news covered and likens his day to fast moving trains. "Once you're done with X, on comes Y and Z is barreling down the tracks" (R. Wilonsky, personal communication, April 24, 2014). The various staffs—metro news, sports, business, and photography—are scattered over two floors. Cuts in the staff have left dozens of vacant cubicles.

Twitter also enhances the social capital ties among the staff is when journalists retweet each other's work. Haag, the education reporter, believes it is important to recognize other people's work by sharing it with others. "I'm retweeting more of city hall reporters and crime reporters because I know them or they write stories that interest me. Part of it is our little network here. We all follow each other. I don't think it spreads as much to other departments." Adds Mervosh, *News* criminal justice reporter: "It can be a validation that you've done good work." She prefers the "more genuine," in person comments. "But it takes two seconds to tweet something" versus walking over to someone's desk.

Peterson, breaking news editor at the *News*, believes Twitter has "improved the comraderie between the young and the old." He said:

> Newsrooms can be so cliquey sometimes. That breaks down the barrier. There is some resistance with old veterans who don't see the point and don't tweet much. But they see it as a way to impart their wisdom or praise on the younger people. And vice versa. The younger, inexperienced will point out a great project someone has worked on. It breaks down those cliques.

Journalists agree that Twitter helps them build better social capital with their readers and colleagues in the newsroom. This is an important bond that helps journalists get validation for their work from peers, bosses and readers. In an era of downsizings, pay freezes, and budget cuts, these kudos are essential to building morale among staffers who have all been asked to do more to make up for those who were let go.

Indeed, Singer (2004) found that reinforcing good work builds on trust between the senior executives and journalists, especially in times of great change. After all, these are newsrooms full of trained skeptics who are always questioning managements' motives.

Journalists have clearly overcome their initial skepticism about the power of Twitter's 140-character messages, which were initially dismissed as fluffy chatter about food. That was a key part of diffusion of Twitter as an innovation—that it is an advantage over existing communication tools. Likewise, Twitter has spread in newsrooms because trusted colleagues tend to use peer pressure to get their friends to try it. This builds the trailblazers' social capital within the news community because they are seen as technology leaders who coach others. By doing so, they strengthen the entire newspaper's use of Twitter.

To be sure, journalists still face fears about what they put out on Twitter because of bad judgment calls by their colleagues. Management, in turn, is struggling with how to enforce guidelines, in some cases, quotas, without it becoming just another burden on the staff. The interviews show there is general agreement that Twitter is a good idea that needs to be used, but it is nearly impossible to enforce strict guidelines on best practices. As editors said, social media effectiveness should be about quality, not quantity, lest it get reduced to a flimsy tally of who's tweeting, as compared to what is being done to actually engage with readers. This speaks to the issue of diffusion of innovation because a new technology like Twitter has to be embraced by senior management if it is going to be adopted throughout the organization. But it has to be observed as being a true improvement over past practices.

FOUR

Does Twitter Make a Difference?

Regardless of the innovation, the bottom line is usually simple: Does it make a difference?

Making a difference can be measured in several ways. The interviews with journalists at the four newspapers show that Twitter is having an impact when it helps bosses recognize their staffs' work. For others, recognition comes when Twitter leads to freelance assignments or invitations to do radio or television shows. For some, it has helped them sell their books. Younger journalists are increasingly cognizant that the ongoing downsizing of newspapers could mean they work for numerous companies instead of staying at one newsroom for decades. This encourages them to curate their own brands, which includes building their own websites and strong social media presences, not just building a clip file from their newspaper work. In rare cases, Twitter is showing promise as a way to build revenues, but editors are still struggling to figure out which social media platform, especially Twitter versus Facebook, will have the most impact on the company's finances

In comparing the four newsrooms, patterns emerged. For instance, all four newsrooms equip their staffs with the latest smartphones, which encourages Twitter, especially from the front lines of reporting. And it has created a 24/7 nature to the staffs' jobs. Interestingly, most staffers do not seem to resent that. Instead, they embrace it as a new requirement of being the best digital journalist who is on top of his or her beat. Editors tend to rely on reporters to be the most active on Twitter, while they retweet the good work of their staff. All four newspapers became active on Twitter around the same time in 2009, with some reporters getting involved earlier. All four newsrooms have hold-outs among the staff who, for whatever reasons, just do not care to engage in social media. All four newsrooms have shown leadership in social media, but to varying degrees. Riley at the *AJC* and Moore at the *Post* are the most active of the four newspaper editors. And those two newsrooms seem to experiment the most with new story formats or being at the lead in using Twitter for breaking news.

To be sure, each newsroom faces financial pressures from owners, especially the *News* and the *Post*. The *AJC* clearly has the greatest freedom as it is owned by the family-controlled Cox Enterprises. Insiders say the Cox's auto operations—Manheim auto auctions and the online trading sites—are the company's cash cows. The same goes for its vast cable company holdings. To be sure, the *AJC* has endured deep cuts as the owners still demand a return on investment. But there is still plenty of investment in new technologies, such as research with Georgia Tech on new digital reporting tools.

Despite its independence, the *Times* has been under a growing amount of financial pressures, even borrowing money for the first time in its history and selling off assets, such as *Congressional Quarterly* and even parking lots.

The *Post* and its staff operate under the specter of always wondering if the paper will have a new owner. Editors openly tell reporters to assume that the place is always for sale, given the nature of Wall Street investors always looking to make a buck. But it is clear that the uncertainties have not deterred great journalism, as seen in the *Post's* award-winning coverage of the Aurora theater shooting.

One of the ways to gauge the impact of Twitter on journalists and their organizations is how it produces any tangible changes in their standing, either in a community or their individual status. This capital takes three forms: economic, cultural, and social. Economic capital refers to anything that can be converted into money or other tangible things, such as property rights. The second form is cultural capital which can take the form of an advanced education, the sum of knowledge, and, helps people enhance their positions in a society. It can in certain circumstances, be converted to economic capital. And, finally, social capital, which is made up of social obligations or connections (Bourdieu, 1986).

Capital inside a newsroom can be improved in a variety of ways. For instance, reporters and editors work together to produce more content for the Sunday print edition. They all benefit because that effort makes the Sunday paper more attractive to readers, which, in turn, attracts more advertisers who want those readers to buy their goods. In terms of a social media platform such as Twitter, building cultural and social capital means building a group of followers. This, in turn, can mean a reporter's stories are retweeted to a greater universe of the followers' followers. This brings greater recognition to both the newspaper itself and the individual journalists. As Kumar explains, "actors in the world of social media and blogs acquire social capital, similar to circulation in the old media, by building their following and friends" (2009, p.154).

To understand how capital is developed in a newsroom setting, it is helpful to review what scholars have previously found in studies of the media. Couldry (2003) used capital theory in the context of studying the media, arguing that scholars cannot study media in isolation because they are both mechanisms and sources of the broader societal framework. He sought to broaden the discussion of the media's social impact and power beyond the individual players and institutions. Bourdieu frequently talked about the journalistic field in terms of how the media impact social realities. For instance, the media's power as a form of meta-capital that means television, newspaper, and radio exert power over other fields, such as education or politicians. If a topic in education gets more coverage by the media, it has increased capital. Benson (1999) described one aspect of the media's capital as its power to "consecrate" a person, event, or idea. "The extent to which a particular medium or media enterprise is able to exercise such consecrating power is an indicator of its relative weight within the field" (p. 469).

Benson's (1999) essay about social capital and the media emphasized the importance of studying the links between news organizations and audiences and how the media are transformed. The media play a role as mediators and explain other fields, such as economics and politics, then share those findings with the public. Demographic changes within the media field are an important aspect of its study, Benson asserted. For instance, increased competition for scarce jobs makes journalists more cautious about what they do. It is also important to consider newcomers' socioeconomic backgrounds, such as where did they go to school and how did they rise in the organization?

Benson (2006) offered a clear description of how capital is measured in media companies. In the journalistic field, economic capital is expressed as circulation or advertising revenues, or audience ratings. In the digital age, however, this measure would have to be expanded to look at page views of websites via tablets, laptops, and mobile phones.

Cultural capital is recognized with Pulitzers and other awards. There can be a conflict because some publications such as *Mother Jones* embrace literary journalism of longer pieces, making them culturally rich, but they are economically poor. Television is a cash cow in the media world, but it lacks the depth to be considered culturally rich. Only a few, such as the *New York Times* or the *Wall Street Journal*, achieve both, which also gives them the prestige and power of setting the tone for all other news organizations.

Duval's (2005) study of the French business press used a number of indicators to measure economic capital. For instance, form of ownership, financial links to other media outlets, size of audience and advertising revenues. The research used a second set of variables to measure symbolic capital shown in location of main office, the publication of signed editorials, leadership by a journalist, and the number of staffers who gradu-

ated from a prestigious journalism school. Benson noted there is no defin-
itive list of indicators to explain the entire news organization, but using
both economic and cultural measures is more precise than just measuring
a media company by its ownership or ad revenues.

In the journalistic field, the measures of capital has been impacted by
the increased gulf between the haves and the have nots. Benson argues
that this polarization has meant more pressure on making money and
creates greater distance between journalism and everyday issues impact-
ing poor people. He cites the increased cooperation between newsrooms
with advertising and marketing departments, which used to be taboo.

To further enrich the understanding of how social capital is impacted
in newsrooms, it is helpful to look at what scholars have found out about
social capital in other settings, such as schools and towns. Each of the
studies outlined here show how strong bonds, or increased social capital,
between members of a community allows individuals to rely on others
for information, relationships, training or jobs (Paxton, 1999). In terms of
adoption of new technologies, scholars use social capital theory to show
how relationships within a community, whether a company or town, can
be tapped to cope with changing technologies (Bourdieu, 1986). Those
bonds of trust help people work together. If you trust your colleague, you
are more likely to help him, and vice versa. Individuals must believe they
are invested in the process before they are willing to try something new
(Bourdieu, 1986).

Journalists measure the impact of Twitter on their social capital by
counting how many followers they have accumulated since joining the
social media platform. Many reporters interviewed for this study were
proud to share the number of followers they have on Twitter, and to
boast just a bit about how they stand against their colleagues inside and
outside their newsrooms. It has become a point of professional competition in which Twitter followers become part of a journalists' social and
cultural capital. Traditionally, a journalists' capital was accumulated
from awards, raises, promotions or new jobs at bigger news organizations. These signs of increased capital are still used, but in the digital age,
capital is also accrued by reporters' presence and activity on social media
platforms like Twitter. And the currency on Twitter is how many followers they have.

"I have over 10,000 followers and I've brought attention to the *Star-
Telegram*. I was one of the earlier people on Twitter and helped make us a
'go to' source," Kennedy said. Joy Tipping, staff writer for the *Dallas
Morning News*, recalls seeing a colleague's Twitter following grow to
2,500 people, provoking her friendly rivalries. "That just ticked me off,"
Tipping recalled. "You are not going to have more Twitter followers than
I do." She tells this story with a hearty laugh, almost mocking herself and
the idea that the number of followers really matters. She emphasized that

she really was joking as she was competing with a friend. (J. Tipping, personal communication, April 23, 2014).

Bill Adair, founder of the *Times'* PolitiFact website, noted that, as of mid-April 2014, the site had 168,000 Twitter followers. His two competitors—Glenn Kessler's The Fact Checker on washingtonpost.com and factchecker.org—have just 10,000 followers and 62,000 followers, respectively. "That's because we use Twitter in a much more expansive and creative way," Adair said (B. Adair, personal communication, April 9, 2014). Perhaps the ultimate recognition for Adair, his PolitiFact team and for the entire *Times* newsroom came in April 2009 when they won the National Reporting category of the Pulitzer Prize for their coverage of the 2008 presidential election. The prize marked the first time that the Pulitzer was awarded for content published on the web before it appeared in the print edition. "A journalist who doesn't have a basic familiarity with Twitter is at a real disadvantage," Adair said. This shows that journalists who now in the position of hiring younger journalists value the role of social media in journalism, and that not participating is no longer an option if you want to succeed in the profession.

Being on Twitter helps reporters build a brand name that extends well beyond the typical identification of the newspaper where they work. This form of social capital allows reporters to build a reputation beyond the typical geographic boundaries defined by a newspaper's circulation area. Now, their work can be tweeted around the globe and establish them as experts on their beats. The number of retweets is another measure of the impact Twitter is having on journalists' capital. For instance, when the Atlanta Braves baseball team announced in May, 2014 that the team was moving out of its downtown stadium for a new ballpark in neighboring, more suburban Cobb County, real estate development reporter Trubey snapped a picture of the architectural renderings at the Braves' press conference and tweeted it out. It was one of the top retweeted stories that week with 170 retweets. "I've never had one retweeted that often," he said. His previous best was perhaps 24 times.

Twitter's biography page allows journalists to introduce themselves to the public, define their beats, and even boast a bit about their level of expertise. Indeed, Kennedy at the *Star-Telegram* describes himself on Twitter as: "Texan at large." And his tweets reflect his belief in covering everything that's going on. He recalled a shooting at a local Navy shipyard.

> When the suspect's name first came out, I looked at the picture and realized that he had waited on me at a Thai restaurant. I tweeted that and that night I'm on Anderson Cooper talking about how he waited on me at a Thai restaurant. It's amazing that Twitter goes from zero to 60 in no time flat. It's lightning in a bottle. That has happened two or three times. Just an amazing thing. I've had a great time. Twitter has

made me something other than an old fuddy duddy by using skills I've always used. And I still get excited about news.

Getting recognized by a national news show confirmed that Kennedy is a known quantity on Twitter, even if it is for something completely unrelated to the news he typically covers. And that confirms his belief in the reach and speed of Twitter.

Times business columnist Trigaux sees his Twitter activity as a way to broaden his reach as a journalist by curating the best of what he reads. By doing that, he figures he is showing his followers the breadth of his interests and that he is truly interested in sharing all sources of information with them.

> I will discuss what appears somewhere else. It might be a darn good piece or we haven't covered it. That brings attention to it even if it's at a competing paper . . . There's an army of smart people out there watching what's going on in Washington, New York, overseas, university and research think tanks, activists' groups and legal firms. It is as much a cross slice of world as you want it to be.

Trigaux is clearly interested in sharing the best work, regardless of whether it is his own, because he wants to enrich the conversation about business and the economy. Indeed, his work has been recognized with national awards, further cementing his position as one of the leading voices on financial news.

These journalists also build their social capital by deciding which pieces they write should be tweeted, as opposed to the newspaper's website, where other editors pick their favorites and give them prominent display. They clearly enjoy the sense of having more control and being empowered to distribute the news, instead of being at the mercy of others who make those decisions. "It offers me a platform to promote myself and my work and colleagues' work," said *News* reporter Mervosh. "I can't control the front page or the home page. Even if the web people don't think my stuff is good enough for the home page, I can put it on Twitter."

SOCIAL CAPITAL TRANSLATES TO ECONOMIC CAPITAL

Times environmental reporter Pittman is an example of how Twitter has improved his social capital and turned that into economic capital. He uses Twitter to monitor what other environmental reporters are covering. Sometimes, he uses Twitter to correct inaccuracies. In April, he wrote a story about a turkey hunter claiming that he was attacked by a Florida panther. "That would be first since the 1800s," Pittman said. His story included quotes from the state's fish and wildlife commission saying they could not verify the hunter's claims as any wounds had healed and there were no visible tracks to show a panther had been roaming the area. But an alternative weekly newspaper in Miami ran the hunter's claim without questioning it. Pittman tweeted the Miami newspaper, resulting in that publication's fixing the story. "This has happened a couple of times," he said.

Pittman also finds Twitter helps him keep on top of what his peers in the Society of Environmental Journalism are writing. Beyond that, several filmmakers now follow his work via Twitter. One of his Twitter accounts is about weird news from Florida. For instance, he tweeted about a runaway kangaroo in Pasco County, Florida. The local sheriff tried to Taser the stray varmint, but it didn't stop it, prompting one of the deputies to jump the kangaroo and wrestle it to the ground.

"That was the same week that the Tallahassee police department Tasered a llama," Pittman said. Such tweets got him some freelance work. In the summer of 2013, the editor of *Slate* magazine invited Pittman to do a month-long blog about the state of Florida. "People are paying attention," he said. Attracting that kind of following, well beyond the *Times'* geographic circulation on Florida's Gulf Coast, has clearly benefitted Pittman, both in terms of translating his cultural capital into economic capital of additional, paid writing gigs.

Kruse, the enterprise reporter at the *Times,* has found freelance story ideas from reading Twitter. One came from a link to a Casper, Wyoming news story on Bam Bam, a big horn sheep that had died. He pitched a feature story on Bam Bam to an editor at *Outside* magazine, who had seen Kruse's work via Twitter. "I didn't know him, but he was following me." Other editors have contacted him via Twitter to ask him to write for their magazines.

Tipping, the lifestyle writer, found that Twitter helped spread the word about her "Joy's Jaunts," a weekly column on places to visit around Texas. When the producers from public radio's "A Prairie Home Companion" needed a quick education on Dallas, Tipping volunteered to help them. That led to producers inviting her to be on the show, hosted by Garrison Keillor. "That was my six and a half minutes of fame," she said. "People now hear my name and say 'I heard you on Prairie Home Companion!'" This is an example of how Tipping and others are building their social capital inside and outside the newsrooms. By getting invitations to appear on a well-known, national radio program, her status as an expert on Texas is solidified, which could lead to other benefits, such as freelance articles or book deals.

Journalists are increasingly in tune with viewing themselves as brands, not just employees of a media company. They are getting more adept at appearing on television as well as writing for a newspaper. And Twitter expands that even more. "If my brand is good for business and the business is a struggling business, I'm happy to do what I can to enhance my brand," said Wolinsky at the *News.*

Blaskovich, digital music and entertainment editor at the *News*, tailored her Twitter bio to reflect her aspiration to be the person to go to for information on what to do, eat or drink in Dallas. "It has been a big branding thing for me. I started to embody what I promised on Twitter. I hope the links I provide prove that I know what's going on." In addition, Blaskovich appears on the News' partner television station NBC Channel 5 to do "Sarah's Weekend Picks," her choice of five things to do over the weekend. She takes her brand name seriously and told her husband that she would not change her name after they married. "I'm a digital journalist first. I'm still Sarah Blaskovich." She noted that if someone Googles her married name, they would not find her professional work, but "pictures of me with my husband and dog."

Haag, one of the Dallas schools reporters, notes that his Twitter page is the first thing that pops up if someone Googles his name. "If you want to know more about me or if I apply for a job, the first thing they will check out is my social media presence. I want people to see that I'm part of this next generation of digital news."

Younger journalists clearly have a sense of promoting themselves and their work as an extension of being part of a larger news organization. (Of those interviewed, 14 of the 50 were under age 35.) One reason is the proliferation of personal web pages, often created during their college years. And the harsh reality of seeing so many colleagues fired during round after round of downsizings. As the 23-year-old Mervosh at the *News* explained:

> The *Dallas Morning News* used to be a destination paper; where you work your whole career. I love working here and I am hopeful about the future. But there are no guarantees. I don't know whether the paper will be in five years. I have my own website. That was a conscious decision. It stays with me even if my employers no longer exist.

Reporters have learned the importance of keeping their Twitter name specific to their name, not the paper's brand. "My wish is to never go anywhere else," said Greg Bluestein, *AJC* political reporter and an Atlanta native. "This is something that you can hold on to. It is like a part of you" (G. Bluestein, personal communication, May 19, 2014).

TWITTER'S IMPACT ON ECONOMIC CAPITAL

In newsrooms, economic capital has traditionally been improved and accrued by breaking news before the competition, writing memorable features for page one of the Sunday edition and winning awards, such as the Pulitzer Prize. The newspaper's advertising, marketing, and circulation departments then promote the great journalism to sell newspaper subscriptions or recruit advertisers. Having higher circulation and page views of the paper's website allows the advertising department to charge higher rates because car dealers and retailers want more eyeballs to see their ads.

The challenge for newspapers is to figure out how new social media platforms can build revenue to replace those lost to Craigslist, Google, and Yahoo. The most traditional measure of newspaper success is selling more papers. Leaders at all four papers say it has been difficult to show solid proof that Twitter alone can boost revenues. Only the *Times* could offer evidence that links Twitter to improved single-copy sales — either from sidewalk newspaper racks or retailers — of the Sunday edition. Deluca at the *Times* told a story during the interview:

> On Sunday morning early, we begin to tweet out the really good deals in the newspaper. Coupons for 20 percent off purchase of Publix groceries. We pepper the market with these. The account is called Times-Deal. We see a lift in single copy sales early in the morning. We easily see a lift of 2 to 7 percent as a result of this. That's huge. . . . And we're not writing a check to someone running a commercial on the radio.

The *AJC* is also promoting deals in its Sunday paper by posting advertising on Facebook on Saturday encouraging readers to look for coupons in the Saturday "bulldog edition," which is an extra edition of several sections of the Sunday paper published and delivered Saturday afternoon. So far, Serra said it resulted in a one percent rise in Sunday newspaper sales.

Beyond those two examples, editors could not cite other cases where Twitter and Facebook have a direct impact on actual newspaper sales. While there is little tangible evidence of a direct impact on the purest form of economic capital at newspapers (increased sales), editors emphasized that it is still relatively early to see results from social media. Besides, in the digital age, it is increasingly important that news organizations look at other metrics, such as visitors to their websites. Building traffic to their sites means news organizations can charge more for advertising because any company selling anything from cars to coats wants more eyeballs to see their products. Editors at three of the four papers have seen evidence that Twitter, along with Facebook, area driving more people to their websites. But it is difficult to make complete comparisons among the four papers as editors are skittish about sharing details. Each newspaper offered a different snapshot of results, either year over year, or three months of results. Dallas declined to share specific numbers. Overall, Facebook appears to be still driving more traffic to websites, but Twitter is catching up and growing at an exponential rate.

At the *Times*, social media accounted for more than 7.1 million referrals to its website, tampabay.com, in 2013, an increase of 50 percent from 2012, according to the *Times* year-end report on social media traffic, provided by McDonald. Of that total, Facebook accounted for 3.2 million of those referrals, up 47 percent from the year earlier. Twitter referred 1.5 million people to the site, an 88 percent increase from 2012, according to the *Times*. "The only thing that had changed was putting our social media team in place," DeLuca said. "We're in the very beginning of this in terms of putting energy, focus and real strategy behind it versus the wild, wild west."

The *AJC* declined to share actual page view numbers but said traffic referred by Facebook rose 109 percent compared to 2013. Twitter page views rose 44 percent versus 2013.

At the *Post*, page views from the end of March until the end of June 2014 showed that Facebook accounts for about 3 percent to 6 percent of weekly page views. Twitter accounts for about 1 percent to 2 percent. By far, the biggest driver is direct clicks on a newspaper's URL, while Google accounts for about 18 percent to 21 percent of traffic, according to the *Post*'s Petty. The numbers get sliced and diced numerous ways, but page views is what "advertisers are trying to get," Petty said.

Editors say they are still experimenting with both platforms to see which one works best for different types of stories. For instance, all editors agree that Twitter is a must for fast-moving breaking news. Facebook is geared for readers who have more time for deeper features. "I think you get a lot better, genuine interaction with the community on Facebook," said Dave Burdick, deputy features editor of the *Post*. Twitter has a breaking news feel and Facebook people are "going in there in a more leisurely frame of mind" (D. Burdick, personal communication, May 28, 2014).

Facebook is showing strong early results on an *AJC* test product for Atlanta Braves fans. In about three weeks, the Braves page attracted 10,000 likes from Facebook users. Another reason is the paper's research shows that Twitter users are "head skimmers," meaning they just read a headline and do not necessarily click through to the actual story on the website. This is evident in the most popular stories clicked on via Facebook versus Twitter. For instance, one of the top five stories clicked on via Facebook was the *Times*' feature on an orphan looking for a family at church. On Twitter, one of the top stories referred were two breaking sports on baseball.

A somewhat controversial blurring of the lines between advertising and news is on the horizon as the *AJC* tests sponsored content, such as a freelancer contributed story on 10 reasons to bring film and television production projects to Atlanta. "Readers don't care" who wrote it, Serra said. Perhaps but it marks a major change in traditional boundaries that separated news and advertising departments at U.S. newspapers.

FIVE

Twitter Changes Boundaries in Newsrooms

Twitter has changed how journalists view their jobs and routines. For instance, the social medium allows anyone to cover any topic that interests them, not just their beat. This can be a great outlet for personal interests and a way to expand their newspaper's limited coverage of some topics.

Consider Jamila Robinson, senior editor for *AJC*'s features and entertainment website. She is an avid figure skater, dating back to her youth in Michigan. While watching the winter Olympics, she noticed that people were talking about the skaters, including reflections and anniversary interviews with Tanya Harding and Nancy Kerrigan, who made headlines when Harding's pals tried to cripple Kerrigan. But Robinson was told by the *AJC* sports editors that people in Atlanta do not follow the winter games. So Robinson began tweeting about the competition, even doing her own video of a "Twizzle" move and an explainer on the judges' scores. "We picked up another 500 followers (on Twitter) because they want to engage with people who know what they're talking about . . . I think it's all about figuring out where the audience is . . . if you get them engaged, they will stick with you (J. Robinson, personal communication, May 19, 2014).

Twitter has also helped change the way beat reporters view the boundaries of their jobs. Consider Jennifer Brett, who covers entertainment for the *AJC*, including any news of new television or movies being filmed in the area. She has realized that beat spills over into traffic patrol because movie crews shut down big chunks of town to shoot scenes. So Brett tweets about road closings, not just celebrities.

When it's snowing, I'm a weather reporter. . . . It is unthinkable to go an hour without posting or checking Twitter. When I go on vacation, I keep up with my people. I feel a great accountability to the people who follow me. I owe them the best around the clock. . . . It has recalibrated the way I think about my job. I have a customer-service mentality. . . . (Twitter) turns your cherished readers into a marketing force. (J. Brett, personal communication, May 20, 2014)

In the spring of 2014, a gunman opened fire at a Federal Express warehouse that was close to where Brett lives, so she went directly to the hospital to start sending out the latest via Twitter. "I'm not a fancy pants, red-carpet glamoratti. I'm a fry cook at the Waffle House. I'm here to serve customers." The proof is in the numbers: 20 percent of the *AJC's* website traffic is referred from Brett's tweets. That "serve customers" mindset is apparent with Dave O'Brien, the *AJC's* Braves reporter. Mark Waligore, one of the *AJC's* managing editors, was at the Braves' opening night and noticed that something was wrong with the American flag. Within seconds, O'Brien tweeted out that the flag had been damaged during the opening ceremony fireworks. "Anyone can get a score anywhere, but knowing what happened to the flag or why the lineup suddenly changed is way more than just getting the score" (M. Waligore, personal communication, June 27, 2014).

Just as Brett sees her role as well beyond her beat, reporters and editors now structure the workflow differently with an emphasis on immediacy, not tomorrow's print edition. Traditionally, a newspaper's production day gave reporters all day to file a story to their editors by 5 p.m. Those section editors usually turned over the copy to the copy and design desks by 7 p.m. in order to make the earliest print deadlines, with the last deadlines held for late sports scores or breaking news for page one.

Now, reporters have to be disciplined about constantly sending out news dispatches, not just producing one story for one deadline. "It has changed the workflow. We are expected to promote our work via Twitter or Facebook," said *AJC* reporter Trubey. He studies the metrics of page views and times of day when web traffic goes up or down. "I prime the pump when news breaks or when people are engaged in Twitter." Traffic to the site is higher in the morning, then drops off and picks up again at lunch time. Traffic picks up again just as people are leaving work at 5 p.m.

We don't have a boss standing over your shoulder editing our tweets as they go out. We're more tapped into our audience than we ever were. We've come out of our Ivory Towers and are getting into the public more so than any time in my career. You are more accountable for the audience you bring in.

The *AJC* has undergone a "shift to an audience-first newsroom," Richardson said. Previously, it was described as digital first to clarify that the audience is "coming from Twitter, Facebook, and print and that's where we have to meet them." Numerous staffers quote editor Riley as saying the newsroom has to cover a story from "Twitter to the Sunday paper." By far, that mantra was the most often repeated phrase during the *AJC* interviews. It is clear that the newsroom has turned itself from thinking of itself as just a daily newspaper to thinking about where is the best and fastest place to get information to readers.

   Doing such additional work beyond the boundaries of a journalists' assigned territory is part of what is helping today's reporters and editors build their own identities beyond the nameplate of their employer.

BOUNDARY THEORY

To understand the application of boundary theory to the adoption of Twitter, it is helpful to first look at what scholars have found about the traditional newsroom structures and hierarchies. One of the historic boundaries within news organizations is the basic organization of the staff. Newsrooms face an endless deluge of topics that could be covered around the clock. Editors have established what gets priority in coverage by establishing beats, such as courts, police, or schools, considered a community's top issues.

   Such beats are generally shaped by geography and topics. For instance, larger newspapers send reporters and photographers to the state capital to cover the governor and legislature. The biggest news organizations do the same with a D.C. bureau to cover the White House and Congress. At metropolitan and smaller-city newspapers, beats routinely include at least one reporter to cover the mayor and city council. Another person covers the police department. Others specialize in topics such as financial news, sports, or education. This way, there is a "delineation of responsibility" for stories (Tuchman, 1980, p. 27.)

   In addition, news organizations create beat structures to routinize news gathering, and bring consistency to coverage. That way, readers know to expect regular dispatches on elections, local employers, and their favorite sports teams (Anderson, Becker, Claussen, et al., 2000). Fishman (1980) found that journalists' routines influence what gets covered. If reporters, for instance, hang out at city hall more often, they are more likely to observe things that then become part of their news report.

   Research suggests that newspapers, regardless of their circulation size, have similar beat structures. Anderson, Becker, et al. (2000) studied newspapers and found that all had courts, police (or crime), education, and hospital beats. Fishman (1980) found that such beats help instill routines and that events are more likely to make it into print if they occur when beat reporters are making their usual rounds and observe the events themselves.

Boundary theory has been used in anthropology, geography, and communications research to look at how boundaries shift and the resulting impact on the people who work or live within those changing lines. One aspect of boundary theory is how forces such as a new technology can shrink or expand boundaries. Any "technological revolution has changed society as well as individual's lives in ways that were never anticipated," according to Hut (1996, p. 178.) Gieryn (1983) defined boundary work as efforts to establish and expand one's domain relative to outsiders. That creates social boundaries that yield more cultural and material resources for those inside the boundaries. Technology has always shaped journalism since Gutenberg invented the printing press, allowing for greater printing and distribution of the Bible (Pavlik, 2000.) Likewise, the introduction of videos had a dramatic impact on television news because it was easier to edit.

As boundaries shift, changes occur. Meyrowitz (1985) examined this in his analysis of the impact of television on social behavior. Television blurred the distinctions between powerful people, such as politicians, and average citizens. Lee (2005) found the role of news sites covering the SARS epidemic blended global and local reporting, breaking the traditional boundary of global and local news.

Lee (2012) used boundary theory to show that the Internet's evolving technologies and increased consumer-friendly tools such as YouTube have eroded the boundaries between the communicator and the receiver, making journalism more of a two-way interaction. Anyone with a video camera or a smart phone can create a video and post it on the Internet, reversing the once-dominant role of television and movie producers.

Lewis (2012) explained that boundary changes are more constant in a field like journalism, especially in the digital age, where the people once defined as the audience now participates through social media platforms such as Twitter. Outsiders re-negotiating the boundaries of journalism may also lead to an evolution of norms and actors, which Lewis (2012) likens to chiropractors filling the void when medical doctors failed to address back problems in their patients. Singer (2015) notes that audience participation via social media platforms also includes a shift in how reporters deliver the news. Traditionally, journalists have gathered all the facts they can by deadline, then focused on writing one story for the next broadcast or print edition of the newspaper. With social media platforms, reporters now tell the story in snippets or build the story as they go along because there is now a greater sense of urgency to get information out quickly (Singer, 2015.) Another shift that Singer (2015) found is in the historic practice of separating the newsroom from the advertising staff. The reason was to eliminate any temptations by the ad sales people to try and influence the news coverage. Journalists have long valued this autonomy as a sacred norm in the profession (Singer, 2015.) Indeed, legendary Chicago Tribune publisher Robert McCormick was so committed to the separation that he created a physical barrier between the two depart-ments. The elevators used by advertising staffers did not stop on the newsroom floor (Kovach & Rosenstiel, 1993). But that is changing as newer journalism enterprises use social media to solicit donations or foundations to support their work.

Robinson (2010) found journalists' boundaries shifted when some re-porters grew to accept the benefit of online comments from readers while others shunned them as extraneous babble. Those more traditional jour-nalists referred to the online forum as the "wild west" (p. 134).

But all accepted that the new digital culture meant a new relationship with their audience that required them to be more interactive. Tradition-ally, journalism has been a one-way street—professionals gather and dis-tribute information and consumers read or view it, and public opinion would develop from those dispatches. This is agenda setting theory in action because journalists decide what's on each day's agenda of news and cover those items deemed worthy of their attention and resources (McCombs & Shaw, 1972). Expanding journalism to be a two-way ven-ture between the professionals and consumers grew with the rise of what many called "public" or "civic" journalism in the 1990s. And this has snowballed with the rise of the Internet and scores of tools that allow anyone to publish information (Marchionni, 2013). Journalists no longer have a lock on the flow of information because anyone with an Internet connection can become a publisher.

WORKING OUTSIDE THE COMFORT ZONES

The changing world of journalism has forced reporters and editors to get more comfortable with different roles, which can include cooperating more with advertising and marketing departments, once considered ver-boten. One of the greatest impacts on news organizations is the arrival of marketing and advertising professionals into the newsroom. This is a huge break from traditional newspapers because of the tradition of keep-ing news separate and insulated from the influence of anyone selling advertising. For many years, the elevators that served the advertising floors did not stop on the newsroom floor (Shaw, 1987).

Indeed, the *Times'* McDonald was a freelance journalist before she joined the *Times* as its first social media specialist. In this role, she leads a multi-department team to develop the entire company's social media strategy. She considers this expansion beyond just writing news to play-ing a more senior role as a strategist to be advantageous. For instance, when I relayed tampabay.com publisher DeLuca's praise of her work—"Amber is one of the brightest young people in the company"—to her, she counted that as one of the benefits to her personal career. McDonald agrees that her prowess with social media will help her get a better job.

Her compensation is not tied to any of the social media measures. "But it has benefitted me. With things like Joe says, that I'm one of the brightest. We are constantly watching our strategy and pushing numbers. We bring people along by having the data. Those are benefits."

Wilkins at the *News* said she has flipped "my thinking" about embracing Twitter as a "marketing function." Indeed, each team in the newsroom reports to an editor, who reports to an advertising manager. It's an unusual structure as most newsrooms keep a solid wall between news and advertising to protect news coverage from any influence from advertisers. "It was a little strange at first," she said of the blending of news and advertising structures. But she adds: "They leave news entirely up to us."

Having this dual news-advertising hierarchy has complicated matters at times. For instance, the *News'* social media team is based on a separate floor from news and is run by people in marketing. Landauer, the digital communities manager at the *News*, said his team has to cater to both advertising and news departments, which he refers to as being in "a hurt locker" between the two. To figure out the right balance of blend of social platforms that are best for the newspaper, Landauer meets weekly with the managing editor and digital editor.

At the *AJC*, the newsroom, marketing and circulation work more closely together. Indeed, the old circulation department is now called audience department. That reflects the shift from carriers' tossing of newspapers into driveways to a 24/7 updating of news on digital platforms. Twitter and Facebook are now the fastest-growing news distribution channels. Perhaps the biggest change was the addition of Michelle Serra as the social media manager. The 27-year-old Serra had worked at a public relations firm that did campaigns for clients such as the U.S. Marines and Pennzoil. She works for the audience department, but sits in the newsroom, causing a stir about whether the business side would try to influence news coverage. Her assessment of the *AJC*'s social media efforts was blunt: "They were doing social media, but not doing it well," she said. Her first day on the job gave her a lesson in breaking news because it was the day of the Boston Marathon bombing. "I had to dive right in and assert myself in the process in a friendly way," Serra recalled. "God forbid if it hadn't worked" (M. Serra, personal communication, May 20, 2014).

One thing she learned before she arrived in the newsroom was the public's enjoyment of the *AJC*'s snarky edge in its tweets. "I told friends I was coming to the *AJC* and they said 'I love their tweets. Don't change that.'" Their feedback showed that there was already a strong, public engagement with the *AJC*'s social media. It appeared to offer her one starting point as she entered a foreign territory of a newsroom. Indeed, she was treated as a foreigner because she was a marketing person plopped down in the newsroom full of skeptical journalists. "News people don't like PR people because there is a sense that they are vacuous, empty people," Roughton said. "She is the opposite. She is rich in content. She is a very gutsy young woman who can own a room. She has the bossy air of a newspaper person." She can "tangle with an old veteran and tear him up. I think news people respond to that."

AJC editor Riley believes the newsroom has to adapt to survive.

> I think newsrooms have to commit themselves to working side by side with people who are experts on attracting people to our digital content and do the things to get the great work we do in front of the maximum number of people. We've never driven circulation trucks out of the newsroom because we had other people to do that. Now we have to be right there with those who are doing the equivalent of that in the digital age.

Just as Twitter has changed the ways reporters gather and distribute information, the social media platform has also changed the old rules about keeping news separated from marketing and advertising. Every journalist interviewed was well aware that the tougher financial times encountered by their own newspaper and the overall industry require everyone to be more nimble for their own survival. Figuring out the best use of Twitter clearly requires putting the best minds together, regardless of old department titles.

TWITTER IS INFLUENCING THE NEWS AGENDA

The interviews with journalists show that Twitter has emerged as a leading part of two big parts of newspapers' coverage areas: breaking news and politics. Given the roles of each paper as the largest in their states, or even the broader region, and in key political states like Florida and Texas, Twitter is now the go-to place for each of the news organizations and has cemented their places as tops in these two top benchmarks of quality journalism.

Natural disasters and mass shootings seem to dominate the news of 2014, and Twitter was a key part of newspaper coverage of fast-moving events. The winter of 2014 was the worst in decades for many parts of the United States. It was especially bad when ice storms crippled Atlanta's major highways, causing thousands of motorists to be stranded in their cars. "By paying attention to Twitter, we became aware of things that were happening around town," Riley said. The challenge is blending both news coverage and using the platform to spread information that helps arm people to be safe or react to changing weather. Weather reports on television are good at that, but "we're not used to doing that," Riley said.

Twitter kept the *Post* ahead of the pack because a night news editor spotted a tweet about a shooting at an Aurora, Colorado movie theater.

The shooting occurred just before 1 a.m. on a Friday, so the morning paper had already been put to bed, newspaper lingo for it was printed and en route to subscribers. "From 12:37 Friday morning until the Saturday morning paper at 6 a.m., we didn't have a newspaper, but you could follow the story on Twitter and you didn't need a newspaper," said Moore, *Post* editor.

Indeed, one of the *Post's* 10 entries to the Pulitzer was the first 96 hours of the Twitter coverage of the shooting. "It's why we won the Pulitzer," he said. Here's the introduction to its Pulitzer entry of the Twitter coverage:

> AURORA THEATER SHOOTINGS. #THEATERSHOOTING
> The *Denver Post* was an early adopter of social media. Our reporters, photographers, and editors understand the tools and are adept at finding sources, information and then leading the competition in pushing those details to our readers. Over the course of the first four days of the shooting, The *Post* and its reporters posted more than a thousand entries on Twitter and Facebook. What follows on the next pages is a sampling of the first 24 hours of coverage. We followed that on day 2 with minute-by-minute tweets as bomb experts disarmed James Holmes' booby-trapped apartment; and then from President Obama's visit and the memorial on Sunday; and finally, from the hearing and Holmes' first appearance on Monday. In between, the people who follow @denverpost and our reporters and editors knew what we knew — immediately.

Moore, who has been in the news business since his first internship in 1974, sums up the impact of social media. "We see ourselves not as a newspaper. We see ourselves as a news organization. It allows us to be in breaking news for real, moment by moment. It infuses news organizations with urgency . . . I can't imagine sitting on a fact until we publish it tomorrow morning. It wouldn't happen. The shelf life of a fact has been reduced to seconds, not days."

The *Post* staff found the Aurora experience has now changed the way they approach news. "We were super, super disciplined," said Coffield, who was then one of the metro editors at the *Post*. To help reporters attending police updates, Coffield would watch the live television coverage of the press conference and tweet out the news. That allows the reporters in the field to concentrate on other angles and stories.

AGENDA SETTING AND THE INFLUENCE OF SOCIAL MEDIA

Scholars first studied agenda setting during the presidential election of 1968. University of North Carolina scholars Maxwell McCombs and Donald Shaw did the first major study to define the agenda-setting role of newspapers and television. It was a time of great social and international turmoil with race riots in cities following the assassination of Martin Luther King, Jr. and protests against U.S. involvement in the Vietnam War.

The researchers interviewed 100 randomly selected registered voters in five Chapel Hill, N.C. precincts about the key issues influencing their votes. In addition, the team analyzed coverage in local and national newspapers, along with Time, Newsweek, NBC and CBS evening news broadcasts. The study showed that the media exerted "a considerable impact on voters' judgments" of what they named as major issues of the campaign (McCombs & Shaw, 1972, 180). The findings have been replicated hundreds of times in other studies about agenda setting (McCombs, 2000).

Agenda setting involves the issue of salience, or what is the most important topic of the day. This is described as first and second levels of agenda setting, or what McCombs (2000) describes as what is prominent on the media agenda becomes prominent on the public agenda. "The media not only can be successful in telling us what to think about, they also can be successful in telling us how to think about it" (McCombs, 2000, 546).

To be sure, the influence of various media outlets changes over time. For instance, the New York Times and local newspapers historically have been the leading sources to set the tone of coverage by others and, therefore, the greatest influence on voters (McCombs, 2000). But in some cases, national television news was more influential, according to scholars (McCombs, 2000).

To understand how the media set the news agenda for the audience, it's important to take a step back and explore who and what influences the media's choices of what goes on each day's news agenda. Historians have shown that journalists set the daily news agenda based on their personal views, routines, outside influences, such as press releases or interviews with sources (Shoemaker and Reese, 1991). Journalists evaluate events based on news value, timeliness, and impact (Tuchman, 1978, Craft and Davis, 2013). In addition, the giant international newspapers, such as the New York Times, have long influenced other smaller publications and television news because the Times as far greater resources to cover more topics and geography (Golan, 2006).

Now, social media is taking its place as a source for mainstream media companies looking for tips on what's going on. As citizens, journalists have turned to social media in their personal lives for information, so it was bound to creep into their professional tasks as well. This is especially true for younger people. Kushin and Yamamoto (2010) found that consumers under age 30 are the most likely to get political information from social media. This has increased as more consumers use smartphones, which make it easier to access social media. A Pew study in late 2014 revealed that 41 percent of Americans use social media to get their campaign news. Social media was viewed by 26 percent as "more reliable information than what is available from traditional news organizations" (Mitchell, 2014). Tumasjan, et al. (2010) studied more than 100,000 Twitter messages about the 2009 German elections to see the social medium's influence. The scholars concluded that Twitter served as a platform for political deliberation.

Twitter has encroached on the professional lock that journalists once had as the keepers of information. Now, Twitter is always on and works as an "awareness system" allowing any users to be up on what's going on, regardless of the time of day or whether a professional journalist is recording the events (Hermida, 2010, 302). A survey of about 1,400 Swedish journalists studied how Twitter has been incorporated into their work. A majority agreed that Twitter offered them tips on stories. Of those who tweeted daily, 76 percent agreed that the audience has gained more influence on media content in the past decade (Hedman, 2015).

A NEW WAY TO TELL STORIES

Twitter has changed the professional norms about how to tell stories. Traditionally, journalists filed daily dispatches on their beats, general assignment duty or a feature. Everyone tries to work on a longer piece for the Sunday paper, which offers more space to readers who are at a more leisurely pace when reading the news. But the 24/7 nature of the Internet changed that mindset and Twitter has made the news cycle even shorter.

Twitter requires reporters and editors to rethink what makes a great story. "It's a different mindset," said Coffield, business editor of the *Post*. The traditional newspaper standard is to reward those who wrote the long, narrative pieces for page one of the Sunday paper. "The Internet doesn't reward us that way." The *Post* is getting a new mobile application and she considers Twitter good practice for writers to learn to write more concisely. "You don't need blathering, long quotes. People are consuming smaller bites" of information.

Indeed, one of the *Post*'s star reporters, Ryan Parker, who just got hired by the *Los Angeles Times*, built his reputation by focusing on Twitter, not the print edition. "He is the person who does not give a shit if something goes in the paper. He just wants to be first to break news." He was named one of Time's most influential people on Twitter.

Twitter has played a key role in digital initiatives at established print newspapers such as the *Times*. Adair was the *Times'* White House correspondent during the Bush-Cheney re-election campaign in 2004. "I determined after the election that we had not done enough fact-checking and we'd let readers down. PolitiFact was born out of my own guilt." PolitiFact is a website devoted to fact-checking claims made by politicians. The site uses a "truth-o-meter" to tell readers whether a claim is anywhere between true and false, which is labeled "pants on fire." Twitter was just a year old when PolitiFact was launched in the summer of 2007. "We realized quickly that this was a great way to reach our audience because people interested in politics were on Twitter early. And journalists were on Twitter early . . . Twitter is like having a crowd of smart people all suggesting things to you."

For *Times'* environmental reporter Pittman, the advantages of Twitter became apparent when one of British Petroleum's wells in the Gulf of Mexico blew up, killing 11 workers and unleashing an estimated 200 million gallons of oil into the ocean.

> The oil spill in 2010 really sort of hit home what Twitter could be used for, particularly in a news setting. We were live tweeting developments on what was going on, tweeting Coast Guard press conferences. There was a lot of interest in those Twitter updates . . . I got a lot of followers off that. I'd guess about 1,000 came from the oil spill. It's like your own personal AP (Associated Press) wire. All that is missing is the bell going "ding, ding, ding."

The massive scope of the oil spill story was a natural for Twitter because "it was happening in a lot of different places at the same time. Louisiana, Mississippi, Alabama, and Florida."

> People had different concerns. What will happen to the beaches and tourism in Florida? In Louisiana, it was the fishing business and also had ramifications for people who are dependent on the oil industry. You could see it all play out on Twitter. I'm not sure a single newspaper story could put all that in. It's an odd thing. . . . It was a mosaic where all the pieces, all the tweets came altogether.

Twitter has clearly expanded the traditional methods of storytelling by journalists at the four newspapers. It has expanded reporters' reach because they can search Twitter to see what others are writing, or to get story tips from readers. This adds to the richness and depth of telling complicated and fast-changing news stories, such as the Gulf of Mexico oil spill. This broadens the traditional view of agenda setting theory because multiple journalists, in multiple markets, are now using Twitter to blend the best information from different sources.

Journalists are enjoying the freedom that Twitter gives them to experiment with new formats for stories. One of the more clever experiments was election day, May, 2014, when Georgia was holding its gubernatorial primary. The *AJC* had its usual fare of lead-up stories, such as a voter's guide and coverage of each candidate's stance on various issues. To mix things up a bit, the *AJC's* Washington correspondent, Daniel Malloy, decided to do a rap song about the election and tweet it out to his followers. "Wake up Georgia, its election day. . . . There's a governor's race, not much to say about it." He did not ask any of his editors for their okay before doing the unconventional report, so they saw it along with his scores of other followers. They thought it was funny and a good sign that reporters are trying to be edgy on Twitter. "It's a sign that we've won the war," *AJC* managing editor Roughton said.

In some cases, Twitter has allowed reporters to go back and recreate a deeper narrative after a breaking news event. For instance, Sarah Mervosh, criminal justice reporter at the *News*, decided the one-year anniversary of the West Fertilizer Co. explosion by recreating the tragic day by using tweets to put together a narrative on what happened that day. "It was a different way to tell a story," she said.

While Mervosh used Twitter to build the narrative for a one-year anniversary of the explosion, editors at the *AJC* decided to write an anniversary story on Hank Aaron's record-setting 715 home runs as if Twitter had been around back in April 1974. The idea came after editors attended a Cox media conference and heard about how other journalists were using Twitter to create narratives. Mark Waligore, one of the *AJC*'s managing editors, came back to work and proposed doing something similar to mark Aaron's anniversary. Tom Stinson, a writer/editor, was asked to do the piece. The paper sent out live tweets at the exact time the homerun was hit, then compiled photos and the tweets for the website. "It created a lot of buzz just because of the coolness of it," Waligore said. He credits Stinson's excellent writing, but notes one reader tweet that said: "Whoever came up with this idea is a genius and should get a raise."

Using photos along with text in Twitter is seen as a way to engage readers further, especially when it is a big story, such as the first news of the US Airways jet making an emergency landing in New York's Hudson River. It became an iconic photo of the pilot's heroism, and, broke the news first on Twitter. Waligore noted the "coolness" factor of recreating Hank Aaron's world record home run. The historical photos were a big part of that because it allowed readers to either relive the big night or show others a major historical event.

Will Vragovic, a photojournalist at the *Times,* uses Twitter to send out shots of key plays while covering the Tampa Bay Rays baseball team, but also for candid shots that would not find their way into the print edition. "I have some control over getting photos out in a timely fashion and in a way that readers can engage with them," he said. Photos are "a universal language. There's that corny expression that a picture is worth a thousand words. I'm not sure what that translated into in characters. But photos speak to people" (W. Vragovic, personal communication, July 25, 2014).

Melissa Lyttle, also a photographer at the *Times*, adds: Tweets with photos "catch my eye. That's a point of entry for me." Besides, they often tell a better story than is possible to convey in the 140-character limit of tweets (M. Lyttle, personal communication, July 25, 2014).

Many of the journalists interviewed view Twitter as their avenue to publish more frequently. Arts critics find Twitter is a powerful tool in helping them stay more engaged with their readers with more frequent dispatches, not just a single review of a production. For *News* movie critic Chris Vognar, Twitter allows him to write about a movie before others without breaking the studios' embargoes on when reviews can be published. He tweets about some aspect of the movie as soon as he leaves the theater. Twitter allows him to publish blurbs of general comments about the movie without "saying it was horrible" and breaking the embargo.

Other arts critics are using Twitter as a different way to review television shows or special events. Stephanie Hayes, arts critic for the *Times*, does a weekly tweet chat with readers during the popular show "Scandal." She did the same to converse and critic the live television performance of "The Sound of Music," with country music singer Carrie Underwood recreating the role of an Austrian nun-turned governess made famous by Julie Andrews.

> You just knew that would be a hot mess from the start, Hayes said. It was so long and agonizing. Twitter was the only thing that got us through it. It made it more fun than just watching it. It has given new life to live TV. Twitter has brought back some of the audience. We all meet up and watch it at the same time (versus the trend of recording shows on digital video recorders.) (Personal communication, S. Hayes, April 7, 2014)

In summary, Twitter has made journalists and their newsrooms more nimble in covering breaking news and politics. Even when the presses are silent in between print editions, Twitter allows journalists to keep readers engaged 24 hours a day. And it is a role that all take very seriously, as seen in the comments about being tethered to their smart phones around the clock, even during vacations, as a service to their readers. This helps journalists build up their social and professional capital within the organization and with the public. Indeed, young journalists are taught that covering breaking news and keeping politicians accountable are two of their biggest responsibilities to the public (Craft & Davis, 2013).

The example of editors and reporters using Twitter in their daily routines shows how the social media platform is changing the boundaries of traditional journalism. Editors are taking on new tasks to free reporters to pursue more information, changing their roles from just production and polishing of final copy to one of gathering information.

The same thing helped reporters covering Colorado's wild fires. Reporters were "out of cellphone range. I'd watch them live" on television and tweet out headlines, Coffield said. Another editor would then assemble those tweets into update stories for the website. "It definitely speeds production. It takes us back to the old days when people would phone it in," she said.

During the spring 2014 mudslides, roads were impassable, but a reporter and photographer biked and hiked into to the area to interview those cut off by the disaster. Even the National Guard had not reached these victims, but the news team "tweeted out photos. It was extremely effective. It got information out to people who were worried about their loved ones," said Laura Keeney, online producer at the *Post* (L. Keeney, personal communication, May 28, 2014).

Besides breaking news, Twitter has given newspapers a competitive edge in how they cover political events. At the *Time's* PolitiFact website, Twitter was key component of the site's coverage of the 2012 Presidential Debates. From a single debate, "we gained thousands of Twitter followers because of the dual-screen effect," said Adair, founding editor of PolitiFact and now contributing editor to the site. "They are watching the debate, following conversations on Twitter, then they link to us and start following us."

> The Holy Grail for fact checking is to do live fact checking. The exact moment someone says something the truth-o-meter says AACK! FALSE! Fact checking usually takes one day or two. But we have this incredible body of work unlike everybody else's. It's in a database structured so you can search fields to find fact checks much easier. (B. Adair, personal communication, April 9, 2014)

Kennedy at the *Star-Telegram* also finds that Twitter is especially useful in a state in a huge territory like Texas, where political coverage is such a big part of the overall news coverage by all outlets. "The state political writers and operatives all follow each other and cross tweet between the Republican and Democratic parties," he said.

For the *AJC*, Twitter has become an efficient way to cover some of the more tedious parts of election day, such as the standard picture of each candidate voting. Instead of taking time out to add each of these to the paper's website, a reporter can simply send it out via a quick tweet. And it is now the go-to source when the Associated Press calls the race, according to Bluestein, who covers the Georgia governor.

SIX

What's the Future
for Twitter in Newsrooms?

The study showed that Twitter is firmly planted as an everyday tool in journalists' pursuit of information and dissemination of news. The social media platform has had a far greater impact than any of the journalists predicted. Most first scoffed at the idea of sending out 140-character messages in a world where news demands context and explanation, not pithy headlines. None of the journalists interviewed initially imagined how Twitter would change their work routines, ranging from a greater devotion to the 24-hour nature of news to experimenting with new forms of storytelling via Twitter. While the use of Twitter has enhanced the economic, cultural, and social capital of individual journalists, it has not done much to improve the financial state of newspapers. To be sure, editors and publishers still embrace it because it appears to be driving more traffic to websites and has improved the organization's overall social and cultural capital with readers. This research makes a theoretical contribution to social capital scholarship because it shows how Twitter builds journalists' social capital, which can then be converted into economic capital.

For an innovation to be adopted, the perception of the functions and the attached values of that innovation become crucial. The research data on how Twitter has been received by journalists at four metropolitan newspapers show that this social medium is embraced as an innovative technology that is becoming a routine part of journalists' daily routines. Reporters find Twitter is both new and better because it provides a good source of information, especially when they cannot be everywhere news happens. For instance, at the *News*, editors use Twitter to monitor what happened overnight by checking tweets by the Dallas Police Department. In addition, reporters at the *News* use Twitter to get fast information from the scenes of natural disasters. The newsroom was getting calls about a tornado hitting an elementary school, but the newspaper did not have reporters posted in that area. By checking tweets from both inside the school and from eyewitnesses, they were able to keep the public up to date on the tornado's impact. This helps news organizations to do their job of getting information out as quickly and as accurately as possible, despite the obstacle of not getting immediate information from emergency management officials. At a time when newsrooms have reduced staffs and budgets, Twitter actually becomes a technological reporting tool that stretches journalists' reach to places where they cannot be.

Reporters have embraced Twitter as an innovative practice. Traditionally, reporters said they could ignore letters or even ringing phones if they did not want to deal with readers. But with Twitter, they feel a closer connection to their audience because they now have a Twitter account with their photo, phone number and biographic information posted for the public to see who is behind the bylines. Readers can click on the follow button and get constant updates on that reporter's work. If people take the time to follow them, reporters said they feel a deeper obligation to answer their questions. "Now you have this crowd of people watching your every move," says Petty at the *Post*. "That's a lot of pressure, but it makes you better."

Likewise, Twitter has given reporters greater reach in their search for sources. Traditionally, reporters worked the phones or went door-to-door looking for witnesses to crimes or sources for other stories. Now, Twitter allows reporters to post a question and send it out to thousands of people within seconds. What used to take hours or days can now take minutes. Consider the *Post's* business staff's search for an owner of one of the autos recalled by General Motors. It was an older model so that meant fewer were still on the road. But they found a Colorado owner, even though he was working at the South Pole.

This helps even when reporters are looking for local people, such as when Hobbs at the *News* was searching for students when a local teacher dismissed after administrators learned she had posed for *Playboy.* Even the school's home phone number directory can be useless because teens rely on cellphones, not their parents' landlines.

Similarly, reporters said it is often easier to get sources to respond to tweets versus phones because busy people can tweet while sitting in meetings and not have to stop their other work to take a reporter's call. One of the interesting responses that reporters cited was this growing dilemma of getting people on the telephone. More and more people are comfortable with smart phones, so they often text instead of call one another. Twitter is an extension of that because it allows for brief exchanges on the go. None of the journalists interviewed will ever completely replace face-to-face interviews with Twitter, but they value it as a supplementary tool in the hunt for people to talk. It is an interesting development to have people more connected than ever through smart phone technology, but they are becoming less likely to actually use it to actually talk to one another.

HOW THE NEWS ORGANIZATION HELPS
OR HINDERS ADOPTION OF TWITTER

Communications channels and an organization's social system can help or hinder the adoption of an innovation. Very few of the journalists said they immediately incorporated Twitter into their daily routines. Instead, they signed up to check it out, then generally forgot about it, often for a couple years. They reconnected with the platform when peers talked about its ease, uses and reach or when they were encouraged by their bosses to become active on either Facebook or Twitter. One of the requirements in Rogers's diffusion theory (1962) is "heterophily" or differences among people. If everyone in an organization is acquainted and up to speed on a new technology, there's nothing to teach one another. But if there are technology leaders in a group, they are often the guinea pigs whom others watch before they try out the innovation. That is the case in newsrooms, such as the *Times*, where former staffer Matt Waite was one of the early adopters of new technologies. His friend and colleague, Craig Pittman summed it up best: "I tend to follow the tech cues of Matt. I let Matt do the Beta test."

As journalists get more active, colleagues compete to see who can gain the most followers on Twitter. Indeed, reporters are very proud to share how many followers they have and whether they are one of the most followed journalists in their newsroom. The *AJC*'s Brett has 30,000 followers and proudly talks that she is second only to the popular sports writers.

In some cases, the most senior editors had to get a nudge from staffers to use Twitter, especially to help promote their work. In Atlanta, *AJC* editor Riley said his paper's bloggers pushed him to take advantage of his stature as editor to tweet about stories. Since his arrival, he has become one of the public faces of the *AJC* through tweets, along with radio and television promotions for upcoming stories. His use of Twitter has expanded because he often uses it to get feedback from readers on issues that he plans to write about in his bi-monthly column.

Just as Twitter allows journalists to find people in distant places, the mobile platform allows them to transmit news from remote places. Consider the *Post's* photographer and reporter trekking into areas hit by mudslides. They hiked and biked into the communities, arriving before the National Guard or other emergency responders. Their tweets from the scene were the only source of news out of the hardest hit communities.

Similarly, Twitter has added geographic reach to disasters that encompass large areas, such as the British Petroleum oil spill in the Gulf of Mexico. The oil slick affected several states' beaches, wildlife, water, and businesses. Having tweets from numerous locations helped journalists' gauge the impact. Readers in turn got a broader scope of coverage by following several news organizations' tweets. Said the *Times'* Pittman: "I'm not sure a single newspaper story could put all that in."

One of the most innovative impacts of Twitter in newsrooms is the creativity it has unleashed in tradition-bound news organizations. Indeed, it is rare to see a Washington correspondent cut loose and do a rap song as part of election day coverage. That's what the *AJC's* Daniel Malloy did, prompting many to retweet it because it showed originality and humor in an otherwise dull election.

Reporters are seizing on to Twitter feeds to recreate scenes to write richer narratives, such as the *News'* one-year anniversary story on the explosion of the West Fertilizer plant. Likewise, the *AJC* could have written a predictable sports feature on the anniversary of Hank Aaron's seven hundred fifteenth home run, but they recreated the entire event as if Twitter had been around in the 1970s, engaging even those who do not follow baseball.

It is clear that journalists need to feel the support of senior management if they are going to feel brave enough to experiment with Twitter. Part of that is the culture of the newsroom. There is a stark difference between the *News* and imposing quotas on using Twitter or Facebook and the other newsrooms. Some at the *News* now view social media as just another task to check off the "to do" list, even guessing at numbers on the monthly reports to their bosses. To be sure, there are curmudgeons in all four newsrooms who still scoff at the need to be on Twitter, resisting any encouragement or quotas.

Journalists appear to respond better to their self-imposed goals, such as the friendly competition to see who can gain the most followers, which is the currency in the world of Twitter. That makes all pay more attention to the platform and builds camaraderie. Reporters who often work in different departments start to form bonds with people they do not see on a daily basis, tweeting out each other's stories, sending kudos when they liked someone's work. Twitter has helped bridge the generation gap at the *News* as younger reporters tweet about a more senior reporter's investigative work, then send the reporter a tweet asking for advice on writing. Peterson, breaking news editor at the *News*, said: "Newsrooms can be so cliquey sometimes. (Twitter) breaks down that barrier."

But every newsroom is still grappling with the boundary of trying to be funny or edgy without offending readers. Some missteps are innocent mistakes, such as tweeting the f-word while watching your team miss a key play during a baseball game. It is one of the downsides of Twitter for journalists—you are forever identified as working for the newspaper when you participate in a very public forum. To the public, reporters have no separate identity, even when using a personal Twitter account instead of their newspaper account.

And the very public nature of Twitter means mistakes are seen around the globe. The *AJC*'s "40 acres and a mule" tweet was an example of bad judgment about sensitive topics such as race. It was picked up on journalism sites such as Poynter.org and jimromenesko.com with comments about somebody will be fired for the error. Editor Riley did not fire the reporter who sent out the tweet and held a staff meeting to reinforce the need for caution when tweeting about sensitive issues, but reassured the staff that he wants the *AJC* to be active on Twitter. Interviews with several staffers showed that his approach allowed them all to exhale because he did not fire the reporter and he knows that being on Twitter is a necessary part of the digital age.

One of the other dangers of Twitter is when journalists get too caught up in the constant deluge of tweets and get too demoralized when readers go on the attack. This is especially true for political coverage when campaign staffers and pundits start ripping apart news coverage. Twitter is dominated by urban and younger people. Hollywood and sports celebrities gain more followers than President Obama (Smith and Brenner, 2012). Even Venezuela's dead president Hugo Chavez still has over 4 million followers on Twitter (Whitefield, 2014). While celebrities and politicians are important influencers of popular culture, trends, and what makes the evening news, Twitter is still a rather insulated bubble, and not representative of the entire U.S. population. That is why PolitiFact editor Adair reminded his staff to occasionally disconnect from Twitter to detox from the barrage.

The flipside of Twitter is when the platform provides reporters with useful feedback from readers or editors. An innovation like Twitter is diffused and adopted within an organization when the innovation is observed by others, according to Rogers (1962). Getting such feedback reinforces reporters' interest in tweeting. Consider *Times*' business columnist Trigaux. He can write scores of columns and not hear anything from readers. But when he uses Twitter to promote his work on Florida's Public Service Commission rolling over and allowing Duke Energy to jack up consumers' utility bills, outraged readers retweet his columns and bombard the PSC with emails and letters.

TWITTER BUILDS SOCIAL CAPITAL INSIDE AND OUTSIDE NEWS ORGANIZATIONS

Twitter clearly improves journalists' networks inside and outside their newsrooms. Building these bonds is part of the impact that Twitter has on journalists and their newspapers. Borrowing the concept of social capital, this study shows that building up a strong following on Twitter is viewed as the currency that matters in the digital age, as compared to the more traditional measure of how many page-one Sunday stories you have in a year. In fact, younger reporters now often ignore traditional standards and focus entirely on their digital work. That's what got Parker at the *Post* recognized as one of *Time's* top 140 Twitter feeds in the country. And, most likely, one of the reasons he landed a job at the *Los Angeles Times*. He is an example where Twitter has improved his social, professional, and economic capital. Establishing himself as an expert at breaking news was recognized by his peers and bosses, which enhanced the *Post's* overall social capital in the community. That translated into his getting a better job at a bigger newspaper, which enhances his professional and economic capital.

For Pittman, his coverage of oddities in Florida, such as the sheriff's department trying to apprehend a kangaroo in Pasco County, got the attention of other publications, which offered him a month-long blog and freelance pieces. He has also built up a reputation as a leading environmental writer because he monitors other publications and tweets out additional information or corrects misleading reports.

Numerous reporters talked about the importance of tending to their personal brands, noting they want to maintain a reputation that is portable and not just linked to one newspaper. All four of the newspapers are considered "destination" newspapers because reporters generally have to work several years at smaller publications before getting hired at such major metropolitan papers. Many people used to spend their entire careers at these papers. But the twenty- and thirty-something-year-olds have seen what has happened to their older colleagues when layoffs hit. They have also grown up as generations where their parents working in any industry were no longer guaranteed a job for life and gold watch after forty years of service. The result is less loyalty to employers and a realization that they, too, may have to move around a few times. Haag, one of the *News'* schools reporters, is proud that his Twitter page is the first thing that pops up if someone Googles his name. "If you want to know more about me or if I apply for a job, the first thing they will check out is my social media presence. I want people to see that I'm part of this next generation of digital news." His colleague Mervosh in the features department puts it bluntly: "There are no guarantees. I don't know where the paper will be in five years. I have my own website. That was a conscious decision. It stays with me even if my employers no longer exist."

Using digital tools to enhance their careers reinforces tracks with what Singer (2004) found when she studied the impact of convergence of television stations and newspaper newsrooms. Journalists learned new skills, such as print reporters learned TV broadcasting skills. Twitter builds reporters' skills because it helps them build their personal brands in the digital world.

One of the impacts of Twitter on the newspapers is the change in culture that embraces new ideas from a younger generation, not just the veterans who have risen to senior management. Social media experts in newsrooms, such as Petty at the *Post* and McDonald at the *Times*, have quickly established themselves as leaders in the digital news age. Both are twenty-somethings and have a great deal of responsibility that typically does not come to youngsters in traditional newsrooms. And both enjoy the respect of the senior most editors. "Hiring Dan Petty and staying out of his way was one of the smartest moves I've ever made," said *Post* editor Moore. This supports research by Huysman and Wulf (2006), who found that organizations must have a supportive culture in order to build the social capital within that community. That means encouraging people to try new things, then share what they know with others. At the *Times*, that included appointing McDonald to head up a social media team to advise the senior management on a cohesive strategy for the entire company. That is similar to what Frambach & Schillewart (2002) found in their research. Innovation is not diffused unless relevant people "buy into using" it.

Newspapers who use Twitter are improving their reputation within the community because the platform is a quicker way to deliver headlines on breaking news. If the paper is known for that, its social and professional capital with readers improves and they are now more loyal to the paper. If they are rewarded with breaking news updates, as well as interesting and informative stories, they are more likely to renew their subscription or bookmark the paper's website. That translates into economic capital because more subscribers or web traffic mean the paper can charge more for print or website advertising.

Earlier research on best practices of Twitter (Swasy & Wolfgang, 2013) found that Twitter is most useful when journalists make tweets smart and engaging and share the best work of other news organizations. The journalists interviewed for this research offered several other best practices that can help other professionals. For instance, Twitter has become a medium that supplements live reporting from breaking news, such as a press conference. Editors can watch the televised event and tweet out headlines, freeing the reporter at the scene to roam around and find other sources and tips. Journalists at these four newspapers are also learning that they can help one another promote upcoming special projects by asking their colleagues with the most followers—such as the AJC's entertainment reporter—to use their massive list of followers to spread the word. This breaks down the traditional silos of topic departments because a well-known sports columnist can tweet about the work done by a colleague in business.

Another best practice that emerged from this research is how Twitter broadens the geographic reach for journalists. Downsized newsrooms no longer staff numerous regional bureaus, which means they cannot cover every event. Instead, journalists are searching Twitter for help when they hear that a tornado hit an elementary school, but no official emergency management agencies are commenting. This allows news organizations to get the best possible updates out quickly to keep the public informed.

It is clear that Twitter has been embraced because journalists' use of it has brought recognition from the highest levels as well. Journalists love prizes. One of the four newspapers in this study received journalism's highest honor for work distributed via Twitter. The *Post's* Pulitzer was awarded in large part for the first 36 hours of coverage of the Aurora movie theater shooting. The shooting happened just as the Friday morning paper was being printed, so journalists had to update readers via social media, then update stories on the *Post's* website. It changed the way the *Post's* editor Moore and his staff think about covering news, with a new emphasis on digital. This recognition by the Pulitzer board suggests that the industry is beginning to embrace short-form, digital work, not just the epic investigative pieces in the *New York Times*. Receiving such a prestigious award that specifically cited the *Post's* Twitter coverage further validates Twitter's role in journalism. This aids in the diffusion of Twitter inside these four newspapers, as well as others, because editors study each year's Pulitzer winners for clues on how to structure their entries, as well as for story ideas for future coverage

Twitter is not showing much of an impact on economic capital as measured in traditional metrics of newspapers sold. The one exception: the *Times* has seen a significant rise in Sunday single copy sales when Twitter is used to promote deals and coupons in the Sunday paper. In the digital world, a more relevant measure that drives advertisers is page views of the website. Each newspaper said Twitter is improving traffic to their sites, but that Facebook lately has been driving more traffic for some content. But two of the four newspapers would not share actual web traffic numbers, making it impossible to accurately judge what impact Twitter is having on that metric. It is interesting to note how three of the four newspapers considered their Twitter and web traffic to be proprietary information that they do not want to share. Ironically, the *Times* shared the information and it is clearly in one of the most competitive newspaper markets of the four papers. Atlanta, Dallas and Denver do not have major metro competitors in their home cities, but the *Times* competes aggressively with the *Tampa Tribune*. Perhaps the *Times'* leadership views it as a competitive advantage that belongs in its public media kit to show New York advertising agencies its reach as compared to rival *Tampa Tribune*. The *Times* has reason to show off the numbers as they show tremendous progress in using social media to drive traffic to the website.

Previous research (Ju, 2010) shows that social media platforms Facebook and Twitter were doing little to build traffic to websites, but that was four years ago, so it appears that the papers are making gains. Still, with newer platforms such as Pinterest gaining users, the jury is still out on which one will be the most useful in terms of building revenues.

The bottom line as to why a new innovation such as Twitter is considered is what it will do to enhance a company's bottom line. If senior management did not see an ultimate economic return, it would not get much backing from them. It is clear that Twitter is delivering an economic return to individual reporters in building their brands. And it is showing evidence of driving traffic to websites so senior leaders will continue to support it.

What is clear from this study is that Twitter is a very useful tool to quickly gather and share information. And it has played a surprising role internally and externally as a catalyst for journalists to broaden their networks and boost their careers.

This study contributes to a relatively new body of research on Twitter, which started in 2006. Others have done research on how news organizations use Twitter, but this study used four theories—diffusion of innovation, social capital, boundary, and agenda setting theories—as the framework for the study. The research shows the importance of social capital and social networks in the diffusion process. For instance, opinion leaders can be both editors and technologically-savvy colleagues, who coach their friends and peers on how to make the most out of Twitter. Editors who show they are willing to break from tradition and let reporters experiment with Twitter see great results—such as the *AJC's* retelling of Hank Aaron's record-breaking homerun. And they are creating a culture that, despite some missteps, encourages even the Washington correspondent to do a rap song as part of his election day coverage.

This study also builds on diffusion of innovation theory because it shows how those who initially resist adopting Twitter are quick to change their minds as soon as they see the benefits. This was a surprise because many innovations are not adopted if they are initially rebuffed. The difference with Twitter is journalists can see fast results, such as their work being retweeted or a growing list of followers, which reinforces their decision to participate on the social medium.

This research also shows how adopting an innovation can have immediate global implications. When reporters embrace Twitter, they are building their social capital inside the newsroom, but also in professional networks of journalists, with readers and people who have never subscribed to their newspapers. In addition, the adoption of Twitter dovetailed with the explosion of smart phones, which allow for greater mobility because of the digital application for Twitter. This is an important offshoot of diffusion theory because it shows another factor in the spread of the innovation: other technologies that will enhance and speed up diffusion. Twitter was already compatible with existing desktop computers, but smart phones have taken it to another level of easy use, 24 hours a day. This has another impact on journalisms and a greater sense of urgency about being first with the news. As one reporter said: "If you don't have it first on Twitter, you do not have it first."

These findings provide new insight for both scholars and professional journalists who are trying to understand how the phenomenon of Twitter can improve news gathering and promotion of content to further engage with readers. Twitter has created a new reporting model and altered the agenda-setting structure inside newsrooms. Traditionally, reporters would gather the facts, return to their desks and write a story for the next day's paper. The next change was the addition of news websites, which meant they filed a shorter version of their print story online. But that has changed because Twitter is now the first place for reporting news. Reporters send out a steady stream of tweets, then write a short web story and continue reporting and tweeting. The print edition story is often the last thing they do. Interestingly, some reporters go back to their tweets to use them as their notes to assemble that print story.

Twitter has also caused seismic shifts in the culture of a newsroom's hierarchal structure. Now twenty-somethings are in leadership and editing roles, directing their colleagues on how to get the most out of social media. Traditionally, journalists had to work ten years before they moved into editing positions, but senior leaders now say putting the millennial generation in charge of social media strategies was the smartest thing they have done.

One interesting result of Twitter's popularity is the impact on newsrooms when someone sends out an inappropriate tweet, such as the AJC's tweet about 40 acres and a mule. Such episodes cause senior editors to pause and counsel staff about what is appropriate use of Twitter. In some cases, newsrooms then held training sessions to broaden the discussion, which has a greater impact of increasing the cultural sensitivities of journalists. Indeed, one editor said he worried most about the "internal combustion" inside the newsroom after such blunders more than the public's scorn. The public forgets and moves on; journalists will watch a senior editor's every move and judge his or her reactions for years to come.

Social media platforms such as Twitter are now part of journalism. What remains to be seen is how they evolve and how news organizations evolve with them. Journalists in this study all agreed on one thing—Twitter is a channel to help new and existing readers find good journalism. Regardless of what technology pops up in the future, the most important role they play is to keep producing accurate and timely reports for any platform.

Every study has its limitations. While the study was enriched by data from 50 journalists in four newsrooms, it would be strengthened further by a deeper, more sustained ethnography based on longer periods of observation of both individual reporters working and the overall rhythm of the newsroom to see how Twitter blends into their routines. The study was conducted at a time when news organizations are still struggling to adapt to a digital world where the Internet has taken away many of their revenue streams, such as classified advertising. As newspapers try to balance their commitment to print subscribers, they are also trying to figure out the best social media platforms that will drive traffic to their websites, which then attracts more advertising revenues to support good journalism and investment in the future.

From a theoretical standpoint, the study was limited because it proved difficult to substantiate specific economic capital gains for news organizations because of senior management's reluctance to share specific numbers. Only the *Times* could show specific impact of use of Twitter on increased Sunday single copy sales. To be sure, there are multiple efforts to improve revenues at any given time, so it is often difficult to separate out what growth came specifically from Twitter, versus, say, a new advertising campaign that persuaded more people to try the newspaper.

The fast-moving digital world offers many opportunities for future work. For instance, scholars should do more on the phenomenon of reporters becoming their own brands, not just newspaper employees, and how that influences their careers. Another rich vein to be explored is the addition of marketing experts to the actual newsrooms. This is a huge break from the tradition of keeping the two completely separate to avoid any advertiser influencing news content. As news organizations search for new business models to generate new revenue, they are likely to try and do more experiments with sponsored content on social media, which raises questions about where are the new boundaries to keep journalism first.

Epilogue

Twitter has persuaded even the most skeptical journalists to sign up for a world of 140 characters or less. Tweets are the new Rolodex to a global directory of sources and story tips. The social media platform has transformed the traditional boundaries of beats and publishing patterns. With this comes more freedom and responsibilities for journalists.

Reporters are building their own brands by tweeting out their own work, which builds their social capital as an expert on their beats, and makes them more marketable in the digital age. This, in turn, speeds up the diffusion of an innovation like Twitter because colleagues pay close attention to what their peers are doing and want to emulate their success and enhance their own social and economic capital.

The economic impact of Twitter is proving elusive as senior management experiments with different social platforms. Twitter is definitely boosting traffic to their sites. And newspapers are building their professional capital because Twitter is the fastest way to spread breaking news, which is essential in times of natural disasters or mass shootings.

Figuring out the balance of various social media in the context of both building new readership, revenues, while tending to those readers who are established with the print edition is quite a juggling act. Part of that is continued testing of Twitter, Facebook, and other emerging social media platforms.

"Facebook is a more productive avenue," said Riley, *AJC* editor. Readers are more likely to click through to our content. Twitter appeals to journalists because it's just like the AP wire. To be sure, it is essential to grow the younger demographic and Twitter is a way to "get stuff in front of them."

In most cases, editors embrace Twitter as a way to improve relationships with the audience and reach those who are not subscribers. In 2016, the Tampa Bay Times saw the impact of Twitter when its reporters covered the Gawker vs. Hulk Hogan trial, a spectacle that attracted international coverage. "We were able to own the story as an authoritative source, being liked to from various sites, thanks to Twitter," said the Times' McDonald, the digital audience manager. Twitter traffic at the end of the first quarter of 2016 was up 37 percent compared to 2015.

DeLuca, publisher of the *Times'* website, views it as a key to survival: "We've got to use Twitter and the next thing after that to engage with our audience. When the next generation is ready to consume local news, we'll be ready to hand it to them," DeLuca said. And the Times audience got even bigger, thanks to the spring 2016 acquisition of the Tampa Tribune, its long-time rival newspaper.

Keeney, online news producer at the *Post,* believes that part of building a new generation of readers is being more personal with them. Millenials are used to interactive experiences with their news and information. They are constantly engaged in using their mobile devices, especially smart phones, to constantly be in touch.

> Twitter is allowing us to have a one-on-one engagement with our readers. We tended to hear a lot of negative things from our readers—the paper didn't get delivered. Now we're asking them to send us pictures or tell us about what's happening. I think it adds a layer of humanness to the paper. It allows our readers to know that we are real people who are dedicated to doing a good job for them.

With the ongoing growth of social media platforms, editors and reporters from all four newspapers continue to experiment to see what makes a difference in terms of gaining audience.

At the AJC, website traffic referred from Facebook soared 645 percent in 2015 versus 2014, while Twitter climbed just 16 percent. The company realigned its team to focus more resources on Facebook to grow it as a distribution channel.

In the newsroom, the digital department was disbanded and those producers were dispatched to each content team, such as the government or business teams. That way, each team has someone thinking about how the story should unfold across digital platforms from the idea conception stage, not as an afterthought.

> "The first news meeting of the day is now at 8 a.m. instead of 10 a.m. We used to sit down, read budgets and everyone was performing for management," Roughton said. Now they do an early meeting . . . "I just listen. The purpose of the meeting is to be clear on what we're doing. We are off and running earlier. Truth is it should be about 6 a.m. We have a huge digital audience around 7 a.m. We have begun to have a night meeting to plan for that. By 8 a.m., we can see what's trending."

Riley gave Roughton the mandate to design the newsroom of the future. A big part of his research focused on other industries. He uses the example of Netflix that started as a company that shipped DVDs. Now it's shifting toward a digital company that does original programming, such as the popular "House of Cards" series.

"They ask questions like why does this TV series have to be 30 minutes? If you hear enough people talk about that and all the paradigms others are willing to break, it gets into you."

In the case of the newspaper world, he asks: "Why do we have to think of everything as an article. " He wants to do more with data visualization, maybe games or quizzes. "We have this notion that we do things the way we've done it before. We're one of the few businesses that thinks that way."

By Spring of 2016, Twitter celebrated its tenth birthday, with journalists making up accounting for a large chunk of its regular users. Still, journalists at the four newspapers interviewed for this 2014 study report they are still trying to figure out the right combination of social media tactics to make the most of the ever-changing landscape.

Indeed, the social media strategy—along with just about everything else—inside the Dallas Morning News was completely revamped after the arrival of a new editor and managing editor. Journalists were reassigned to new jobs and its internal report on its plans said the organization "urgently needs sweeping change" (Hare, 2016).

Likewise, management at the Denver Post was changing with the resignation of editor Greg Moore in the spring of 2016. Petty, now director of audience development at the Post, said the newsroom has beefed up its production of videos, including thirty-second "teasers" for Facebook because videos get a higher priority on that platform. He said about 75 percent to 80 percent of the Post's traffic in 2016 comes from Facebook, compared with 15 percent to 18 percent from Twitter. But the bulk of referrals—more than 40 percent at times—comes from search engines. That's great to have readers see the paper's content, but the challenge remains how newspapers are going to make money. One estimate put it bluntly: 85 cents of every digital dollar spent on ads in early 2016 was going to Google or Facebook.

Regardless of changes in the digital world, journalists agree that it still comes down to doing quality work. If readers click through on Twitter to find mediocre content, they will not come back. Inside the *Times*, everyone from the circulation truck drivers to the advertising sales representatives learn from day one that there is nothing to deliver or sell if the news report is not the very best. The saying is "news drives the train."

"What we do is local news with journalistic credibility," said DeLuca, *Times* website publisher. "The need for that will be forever."

References

Ahmad, Ali Nobil. 2010. "Is Twitter a Useful Tool for Journalists?" *Journal of Media Practice* 11:145–55.

Alden, William. 2013. "Opening With a Pop, Key Moments From Twitter's First Day of Trading." *New York Times*. November 7. http://dealbook.nytimes.com/2013/11/07/live-blog-tracking-twitters-i-p-o/?_r=0.

Anderson, William, Becker, Lee, Claussen, Dane and Lowrey, Wilson. 2000. "Why does the bet go on?" Newspaper Research Journal 21 (4): 2-16.

Arceneaux, Noah, and Amy Schmitz Weiss. 2010. "Seems Stupid until You Try It: Press Coverage of Twitter, 2006–9." *New Media & Society* 12:1262–79.

Armstrong, Cory L., and Fangfang Gao. 2010. "Now Tweet This: How News Organizations Use Twitter." *Electronic News* 4 (4): 218–35.

Bagdikian, Ben H. 2004. *The New Media Monopoly*. Boston: Beacon Press.

Barnard, Stephen R. 2012. *Twitter and the Journalistic Field: How the Growth of a New(s) Medium is Transforming Journalism*. Unpublished PhD dissertation. University of Missouri, Columbia, MO.

Beam, Randall A., David H. Weaver, and Bonnie J. Brownlee. 2009. "Changes in Professionalism of US Journalists in the Turbulent Twenty-First Century." *Journalism & Mass Communication Quarterly* 86 (2): 277–98.

Benson, Rodney. 1999. Field theory in comparative context: A new paradigm for media studies. *Theory and Society, 28*(3), 463-498.

Benson, Rodney. 2006. "News Media as a "Journalistic Field": What Bourdieu Adds to New Institutionalism, and Vice Versa." *Political Communication* 23 (2): 187–202.

Beaumont, Claudine. 2009. "New York Plane Crash: Twitter Breaks the News, Again." *Telegraph*. January 16. http://www.telegraph.co.uk/technology/twitter/4269765/New-York-plane-crash-Twitter-breaks-the-news-again.html.

Blasingame, Dale. 2011. "Twitter First: Changing TV News 140 Characters at a Time." *International Symposium on Online Journalism*. http://online.journalism.utexas.edu/2011/papers/Dale2011.pdf.

Boyle, Kris, and Carol Zuegner. 2012. "News Staffs Use Twitter to Interact with Readers." *Newspaper Research Journal* 33 (4): 6–19.

Boase, Jeffrey, John B. Horrigan, Barry Wellman, and Lee Rainie. 2006. "The Strength of Internet Ties." *Pew Internet and American Life Project*. http://www.pewinternet.org/pdfs/PIP_Internet_ties.pdf.

Bourdieu, Pierre. 1986. "The Forms of Capital." In *Handbook of Theory of Research for the Sociology of Education*, edited by J. G. Richardson. 241–58. New York: Greenwood Press.

Bourdieu, Pierre. 2002. "The Forms of Capital." In *Readings in Economic Sociology*, edited by Nicole Woolsley Biggart. 280–91. Malden, MA: Blackwell Publishers.

Breed, Warren. 1955. "Social Control in A Newsroom." *Social Forces* 33:326–55.

Broersma, M. & Graham, T. (2013). Twitter As A News Source. Journalism Practice 7: (4), 446-464.

Buttry, Steve. 2011. "Why Editors Should Be Active on Twitter." *The Buttry Diary*. http://stevebuttry.wordpress.com/2011/08/02/why-editors-should-be-active-on-twitter/.

Canter, Lily. 2014. "Personalised Tweeting." *Digital Journalism* 1: 1-23.

Carr, David. 2010. "Why Twitter Will Endure," *New York Times*. January 1. http://www.nytimes.com/2010/01/03/weekinreview/03carr.html?pagewanted=all.

Cobb, James C. 2013. Lewis Grizzard (1946–1994). *New Georgia Encyclopedia*. http://www.georgiaencyclopedia.org/articles/arts-culture/lewis-grizzard-1946-1994. Cox-enterprises.com. 2014.

Couldry, Nick. 2003. "Media, Symbolic Power and the Limits of Bourdieu's Field Theory." *Media@lse*, London School of Economics and Political Science. London: London School of Economics.

Craft, Stephanie and Charles N. Davis. 2013. *Principles of American Journalism: An Introduction*. New York: Routledge.

Crossman, David M. 1997. "The evolution of the World Wide Web as an emerging instructional technology tool." In *Web-Based Instruction*, edited by Badrul H. Kahn. 19–23. Englewood Cliffs: Educational Technology Publications, Inc.

Dahlgren, Peter. 2009. *Media and Political Engagement*. Cambridge: Cambridge University Press.

Dailey, Larry, Lori Demo, and Mary Spillman. 2005. "The Convergence Continuum: A Model for Studying Collaboration between Media Newsrooms." *Atlantic Journal of Communication* 13 (3): 150–68.

Donath, Judith, and Danah Boyd. 2004. "Public Displays of Connection." *BT Technology Journal* 22 (4): 71–82.

Donohue, George A., Clarice N. Olien and Phillip J. Tichenor. 1989. "Structure and Constraints on Community Newspaper Gatekeepers." *Journalism Quarterly* 66 (4): 807–45.

Doolin, Bill, and Alan Lowe. 2002. "To Reveal Is to Critique: Actor-Network Theory and Critical Information Systems Research." *Journal of Information Technology* 17 (2): 69–78.

Duhe, Sonya F., Melissa M. Mortimer, and San S. Chow. 2004. "Convergence in North American TV Newsrooms: A Nationwide Look." *Convergence: The International Journal of Research into New Media Technologies* 10 (2): 81–104.

Dugan, Lauren. 2011. "Only Three Editors from the 10 Top Newspapers in the U.S. Are on Twitter." *AdWeek*. August 4. http://www.adweek.com/socialtimes/only-three-editors-from-the-10-top-newspapers-in-the-us-are-on-twitter/453751.

Duggan, M. and Smith, A. (2013). Social media update 2013. Pew Research Center. Retrieved from http://www.pewinternet.org/files/oldmedia/Files/Reports/2013/Social%20Networking% 202013_PDF.pdf.

Duval, J. 2005. Economic Journalism in France. In R. Benson & E. Neveu (Eds.), *Bourdieu and the Journalistic Field*, p. 135-155. Cambridge. UK: Polity.

Edmonds, Rick, Emily Guskin, Amy Mitchell, and Mark Jurkowitz. 2013. "State of the News Media, 2013, Newspapers by the Numbers." Pew Research Center's Project for Excellence in Journalism. http://stateofthemedia.org/2013/newspapers-stabilizing-but-still-threatened/newspapers-by-the-numbers/.

Elliott, Amy-Mae. 2013. "9 Breaking News Tweets That Changed Twitter Forever." *Mashable*. http://www.mashable.com/2013/10/31/twitter-news/.

Ellison, Nicole B., Charles Steinfield, and Cliff Lampe. 2007. "The Benefits of Facebook 'Friends:' Social Capital and College Students' Use of Online Social Network Sites." *Journal of Computer-Mediated Communication* 121:1143–68.

Ferguson, Douglas A. and Clark F. Greer. 2011. "Local Radio and Microblogging: How Radio Stations in the U.S. Are Using Twitter." *Journal of Radio and Audio Media* 18 (1): 33–46.

Fishman, M. 1980, The manufacture of news: Social problems, deviance, and the mass media. Beverly Hills, CA: Sage.

Fitzpatrick, Alex. 2014. "The 140 Best Twitter Feeds of 2014." *Time*. May 1. http://time.com/collection/twitter-140/.

Frank, Kenneth, Yong Zhao, and Kathryn Borman. 2004. "Social Capital and the Diffusion of Innovations within Organizations: The Case of Computer Technology in Schools." *Sociology of Education* 77 (April): 148–71.

Frambach, Ruud, and Niels Schillewaert. 2002. "Organizational Innovation Adoption:A Multi-Level Framework of Determinants and Opportunities for Future Research." *Journal of Business Research* 55:163–76.

Garrett, Judith M. and Michael V. Hazel. 2010. "*Dallas Morning News,*" Handbook of Texas. Texas State Historical Association. http://www.tshaonline.org/handbook/online/articles/eed12.

Garrison, Bruce. 2000. "Diffusion of a New Technology On-Line Research in Newspaper Newsrooms." *Convergence: The International Journal of Research into New Media Technologies* 6 (1): 84–105.

Garrison, Bruce. 2001. "Diffusion of Online Information Technologies in Newspaper Newsrooms." *Journalism*, 2 (2): 221–39.

Gelles, David, and Vindu Goel. 2013. "Twitter Raises Price Range for Its I.P.O., *New York Times.*" November 4. http://dealbook.nytimes.com/2013/11/04/twitter-raises-price-range-for-i-p-o/?ref=twitter&_r=0.Georgiaencyclopedia.org. 2004-2015. The Georgia Humanities Council and The University of Georgia Press.

Gieryn, Thomas. F. 1983. Boundary-work and the demarcation of science from nonscience: Strains and interests in professional ideologies of scientists. *American sociological review*, 781-795.

Gillmor, Dan. 2004. *We the Media: Grassroots Journalism by the People, for the People.* Sebastopol, CA: O'Reilly Media.

Golan, G. (2006). Inter-media Agenda Setting and Global News Coverage: Assessing the influence of the New York Times on three network television evening news programs. Journalism Studies, 7(2), 323.

Greer, Jennifer, and Yan Yan. 2010. "New Ways of Connecting with Readers: How Community Newspapers Are Using Facebook, Twitter and Other Tools to Deliver the News." *Grassroots Editor* 51 (3): 1–7.

Habermas, Jurgen. 1989. The structural transformation of the public sphere (T. Burger, Trans.). *Cambridge, MA: Massachusetts Institute of Technology Press (Original work published 1962).*

Habermas, Jürgen. 1991. *The Structural Transformation of the Public Sphere: An Inquiry into a Category of Bourgeois Society.* Cambridge, MA: MIT Press.

Hamby, Peter. 2013. "Did Twitter Kill the Boys on the Bus? Searching for a Better Way to Cover a Campaign." Joan Shorenstein Center on the Press, Politics and Public Policy Discussion Paper Series.

Hare, Kristen. 2016. "At The Dallas Morning News, becoming truly digital means starting over." Poynter.org. http://www.poynter.org/2016/at-the-dallas-morning-news-becoming-truly-digital-means-starting-over/400041/

Hedman, Ulrika. 2015. "Tweeters," *Digital Journalism*, 3(2): 279-297.

Hazlehurst, John. 2014. "Denver Post May be for Sale—Will Anschultz bid?" *Colorado Springs Business Journal.* April 3. http://csbj.com/2014/04/03/denver-post-may-sale-will-anschutz-bid/.

Hermida, Alfred. 2010. "Twittering the News: The Emergence of Ambient Journalism." *Journalism Practice* 4 (3): 297–308.

Hermida, Alfred. 2013. "#Journalism," *Digital Journalism*, 1(3): 295-313.

Herrera, Susana, and José Luis Requejo. 2012. "10 Good Practices for News Organizations Using Twitter." *Journal of Applied Journalism and Media Studies* 1 (1): 79–95

Holcomb, Jesse, Kim Gross, and Amy Mitchell. 2011. "How Mainstream Media Outlets Use Twitter." Pew Research Center's Project for Excellence in Journalism. Retrieved from http://www.journalism.org/analysis_report/how_mainstream_media_outlets_use_twitter.

Honan, Mat. 2013. "*Hatching Twitter* Reveals Dark Side of Company's Brilliant History." *Wired.* November 5. http://www.wired.com/gadgetlab/2013/11/hatching-twitter/.

Hong, Sounman. 2012. "Online News on Twitter: Newspapers' Social Media Adoption and their Online Readership." Information Economics and Policy 24 (1): 69–74.

Hut, Piet. 1996. "Structuring reality: The role of limits." In *Boundaries and barriers: On the limits to scientific knowledge,* edited by J. L. Casti & A. Karlqvist, 148–187. Reading: MA: Addison-Wesley.

Hutto, C.J., Sarita Yardi, and Eric Gilbert. 2013. "A Longitudinal Study of Follow Predictors on Twitter." Paper presented at Computer-Human Interaction annual conference, CHI 2013, Paris, France. April 27-May 13.

Huysman, Marleen, and Volker Wulf. 2005. "IT to Support Knowledge Sharing in Communities, Towards a Social Capital Analysis." *Journal of Information Technology* 21 (1): 40–51.

Johnson, John M. 2002. "In-Depth Interviewing." In *Handbook of Interview Research: Context and Method,* edited by Jaber F. Gubrium and James Holstein. 103–19. Thousand Oaks, CA: Sage Publications.

Johnson, Phillip, and Sung-Un Yang. 2009. "Uses and Gratifications of Twitter: An Examination of User motives and Satisfaction of Twitter Use." Paper presented at Association for Education in Journalism and Mass Communication, Boston, MA, August 5–8.

Ju, Alice. 2010. "Evaluating the Effectiveness of Facebook and Twitter as New Publishing Platforms for Newspapers." Unpublished master's thesis, University of Texas.

Kirchhoff, Suzanne M. 2009. "The U.S. Newspaper Industry in Transition." Congressional Research Service. https://www.fas.org/sgp/crs/misc/R40700.pdf.

Keller, Suzanne. 1977. "The Telephone in New, and Old, Communities." In *The Social Impact of the Telephone,* edited by Ithiel de Sola Pool, 281–98. Cambridge, MA: MIT Press.

Kovack, Bill and Tom Rosenstiel. 2001. *The Elements of Journalism: What Newspeople Should Know and the Public Should Expect.* New York: Random House.

Kumar, Anup. 2009. "Looking Back and Looking Ahead: Journalistic Rules, Social Control, Social Change and Relative Autonomy." Journal of Media Sociology, 1 (3/4): 154.

Kushin, M. and Yamamoto, M. (2010). Did Social Media Really Matter? Students' Use of Online Media and Political Decision Making in the 2008 Election. Mass Communication and Society 13 (5), 608-630.

Kwak, Haewoon, Changhyun Lee, Hosung Park, and Sue Moon. 2010. "What Is Twitter, a Social Network or a News Media?" Paper presented at 19 International World Wide Web Conference, Raleigh, NC, April 26-30.

Lasorsa, Dominic L., Seth C. Lewis, and Avery E. Holton. 2012. "Normalizing Twitter: Journalism Practice in an Emerging Communication Space." *Journalism Studies* 13 (1): 19–36.

Lee, Alice. 2005. "Between global and local: The glocalization of news coverage on the trans-regional crisis of SARS," *Asian Journal of Communication*, 15(3): 255–273.

Lee, Alice. 2012. "Online news media in the Web 2.0 era: from boundary dissolution to journalistic transformation," *Chinese Journal of Communication*, 5 (2):210-226.

Lewis, Seth. 2012. "The tension between professional control and open participation," *Information, Communication & Society* 15(6): 836-866.

Maier, Scott R. 2000. "Digital Diffusion in Newsrooms: The Uneven Advance of Computer-Assisted Reporting." *Newspaper Research Journal* 21 (2): 95–110.

Marchionni D. M. (2013) Journalism-as-a-conversation: A concept explication. *Communication Theory* 23(2): 131-147.

Marquis, Alice G. 1984. "Written on the Wind: The Impact of Radio during the 1930s." *Journal of Contemporary History* 19:385-415.

McCombs, M., Shaw, D., and Weaver, D. (2014). New Directions in Agenda-Setting Theory and Research. Mass Communication & Society, 17(6), 781-802.

McCombs, M. (2000). The agenda setting role of the mass media in the shaping of public opinion. Unpublished manuscript.

McCombs, Maxwell and Shaw, Donald. (1972). The agenda-setting function of mass media. Public opinion quarterly, 176-187.

Messner, Marcus, Maureen Linke, and Asriel Eford. 2011. "Shoveling Tweets: An Analysis of the Microblogging Engagement of Traditional News Organizations." Paper presented at the International Symposium on Online Journalism, Austin, TX, April 1.

Meyrowitz, Joshua. 1985. *No sense of place: The impact of electronic media on social behavior.* New York: Oxford University Press.

Mitchell, Amy, and Emily Guskin. 2013. "Twitter News Consumers: Young, Mobile and Educated." Pew Research Center. http://pewrsr.ch/HqSKYT.

Mitchell, Amy. 2013. Twitter news consumers: Young, mobile and educated. Pew Research Center. Retrieved from http://pewrsr.ch/HqSKYT.

Murthy, Dhiraj. 2011. "Twitter: Microphone for the Masses?" *Media, Culture & Society,* 33 (5): 779–89.

NAA.org. 2014. Newspaper Association of America, Arlington, Va.

Nieman Reports. 2012. *Truth in the Age of Social Media.* Nieman Foundation for Journalism at Harvard. http://niemanreports.org/articles/category/cover-story-truth-in-the-age-of-br-social-media/.

O'Connor, B., Balasubramanyan, R., Routledege, B., and Smith, N. (2010). From Tweets to Polls: Linking Text Sentiment to Public Opinion Time Series. ICWSM 11 (122-129), 1-2.

O'Donohoe, Stephanie. 1994. "Advertising Uses and Gratifications." *European Journal of Marketing* 28 (8–9): 52–75.

Orlinski, Wanda, and Debra Gash. 1994. "Technological Frames: Making Sense of Information Technology in Organizations." *ACM Transactions on Information Systems.* 12 (2): 174–207.

Parmelee, J. H. (2013). Political journalists and Twitter: Influences on norms and practices. *Journal of Media Practice, 14,* 291-305.

Paxton, Pamela. 1999. "Is Social Capital Declining in the United States? A Multiple Indicator Assessment." *American Journal of Sociology,* 105 (1): 88–127.

Pavlik, John. (2000). The impact of technology on journalism. *Journalism Studies, 1*(2), 229-237.

Peslak, Alan, Wendy Ceccucci, and Patricia Sendall. 2010. "An Empirical Study of Social Networking Behavior Using Diffusion of Innovation Theory." Paper presented to Conference on Information Systems Applied Research, Nashville, TN, October 28-31.

Perry, Chuck. 2013. "Atlanta Journal-Constitution." New Georgia Encyclopedia. http://www.georgiaencyclopedia.org/articles/arts-culture/atlanta-journal-constitution.

Pew Research Center's Project for Excellence in Journalism. State of the News Media, 2013. Retrieved from http://stateofthemedia.org/2013/newspapers-stabilizing-but-still-threatened/newspapers-by-the-numbers/.

Poell, Thomas and van Dijck, José. 2014. "Social media and journalistic independence," in *Media Independence: Working with Freedom or Working for Free?,* edited by James Bennett & Niki Strange, 182-201. London: Routledge.

Purcell, Kristen, Lee Rainie, Amy Mitchell, Tom Rosenstiel, and Kenny Olmstead. 2010. "Understanding the Participatory News Consumer: How Internet and Cell Phone Users Have Turned News into a Social Experience." Pew Research Center. http://www.pewinternet.org/Reports/2010/Online-News.aspx?r=1.

Putnam, Robert. 1993. "The Prosperous Community." *American Prospect* 4 (13): 35–42. http://prospect.org/article/prosperous-community-social-capital-and-public-life.

Putnam, Robert. 2000. *Bowling Alone: The Collapse and Revival of American Community.* New York: Simon & Schuster.

Recuero, Raquel, Ricardo Araújo, and Gabriela Zago. 2011. "How Does Social Capital Affect Retweets?" Paper presented at Fifth International AAAI Conference on Weblogs and Social Media 2011. Barcelona, Spain, July 17-21. http://www.aaai.org/ocs/index.php/ICWSM/ICWSM11/paper/view/2807.

Reich, Zvi. 2013. "The Impact of Technology on News Reporting: A Longitudinal Perspective." *Journalism & Mass Communications Quarterly* 90 (3): 417–34.

Reuters. 2012. "USA Today Gets First Significant Makeover in 30 Years." *Chicago Tribune.* September 14.

Rindfuss, Allen. 2009. "The Use of Twitter by America's Newspapers." *The Bivings Report.* http://www.bivingsreport.com/2009/the-use-of-twitter-by-americas- newspapers/.

Robinson, Sue. 2010. "Traditionalists vs. Convergers: Textual Privilege, Boundary Work, and the Journalist—Audience Relationship in the Commenting Policies of Online News Sites," *Convergence: The International Journal of Research into New Media Technologies,* 16(1): 125-143.

Rogers, Everett M. 1962. *Diffusion of Innovations.* New York: Free Press.

Rogers, Everett M. 1976. "New Product Adoption and Diffusion." *Journal of Consumer Research,* 2:290–301.

Schudson, Michael. 1978. *Discovering the News: A Social History of American Newspapers.* New York: Basic Books.

Shirky, Clay. 2008. *Here Comes Everybody: The Power of Organizing Without Organizations.* New York: Penguin.

Shoemaker, P. & Reese, S. (1996). Mediating the Message: theories of influences on mass media content, New York: Routledge.

Singer, Jane B. 2004. "Strange Bedfellows? The Diffusion of Convergence in Four News Organizations." *Journalism Studies* 5 (1): 3–18.

Singer, Jane B. 2010. "Quality Control: Perceived Effects of User-Generated Content on Newsroom Norms, Values and Routines." *Journalism Practice* 4 (2): 127–42.

Singer, Jane, Hermida, Alfred, Domingo, David, Quandt, Heinonen, Paulussen, Steve, Reich, Zvi, and Vujnovic, Marina. 2011. Participatory Journalism in Online Newspapers: guarding the Internet's open gates.

Singer, Jane. 2015. "Out of Bounds: Professional Norms as Boundary Markers," in *Boundaries of Journalism,* edited by Matt Carlson and Seth C. Lewis. London: Routledge.

Smith, Aaron, and Joanna Brenner. 2012. "Twitter Use 2012." Pew Research Institute. Retrieved from http://www.pewinternet.org/2012/05/31/twitter-use-2012/.

Sonderman, Jeff, and Andrew Beaujon. 2012. "Twitter Study: Hashtags and URLs Can Double Engagement." Poynter Institute. http://www.poynter.org/latest-news/mediawire/189021/twitter-study-hashtags-and-urls-can-double-engagement/ #.US0yIJ7L8jI.email.

Swasy, Alecia, and David Wolfgang. 2013. "Best Twitter Practices for Journalists." Donald W. Reynolds Journalism Institute. http://www.rjionline.org/blog/best-twitter-practices-journalists

Swasy, Alecia & Perreault, Gregory (2013). A Commentary Echo Chamber: Twitter as an Information Subsidy in Coverage of U.S. Senate Candidate Todd Akin. Accepted for presentation at International Communication Association annual meeting, London, England, June, 2013.

Tandoc, Edson. 2013. "Web Analytics, Social Media, and the Journalistic Doxa: The Impact of Audience Feedback on the Evolving Gatekeeping Process." Unpublished PhD dissertation, University of Missouri, Columbia.

Taylor, George Rogers. 1951. *The Transportation Revolution, 1815–1860,* New York: Rinehart and Co.

Tsukayama, Hayley. 2013. "Twitter Turns 7: Users Send Over 400 Million Tweets Per Day." *Washington Post.* March 21. articles.washingtonpost.com/2013-03-21/business/ 37889387_1_tweets-jack-dorsey-twitter.

Tuchman, G. (1978). Making the News: A study in the construction of reality. New York: Free Press.

Tumasjan, A., Sprenger, T., Sandner, P., and Welpe, I. (2011). "Electoral Forecast with Twitter: What 140 Characters Reveal about the Political Landscape." *Social Science Computer Review,* 29(4), 402-418.

Van Maanen, John. 1983. *Qualitative Methods*. Beverly Hills, CA: Sage Publications.

Vaughn, Stephen L. 2008. *Encyclopedia of American Journalism*. New York: Routledge.

Vis, Farida. 2013. "Twitter as a reporting tool for breaking news." *Digital Journalism* 1 (1): 27–47.

Weaver, David H., Randal A. Beam, Bonnie J. Brownlee, Paul S. Voakes, and G. Cleveland Wilhoit. 2007. *The American Journalist in the 21st Century: U.S. News People at the Dawn of a New Millenium*. Mahwah, NJ: Lawrence Erlbaum.

Weir, Tom. 1998. "Innovators as News Hounds? A Study of Early Adopters of the Electronic Newspaper." Paper presented at annual meeting for the Association for Education in Journalism and Mass Communications, Baltimore, MD. August 5–8.

Weiss, Amy S. and David Domingo. 2010. "Innovation Processes in Online Newsrooms as Actor-Networks and Communities of Practice," *New Media & Society* 12 (7): 1156–71.

Whitefield, Mimi. 2014. "Want more Twitter followers? Become a world leader." *Miami Herald*, June 27. http://www.miamiherald.com/2014/06/25/4201724/the-world-is-atwiter-as-more-world.html.

Yang, Nu, and Ed Zintel. (2014) "25 under 35." Editor and Publisher. April 4. http://www.editorandpublisher.com/Features/Article/25-Under-352014-04-07T08-35-44.

Index

accuracy: breaking news and, 24; concerns about, 15, 37; using Twitter to verify, 46–47
Adair, Bill, 45, 60, 64
adoption of new technologies: expectations about usefulness, 9; news organizations influencing, 67–69; perception of value, 65; social capital theory and, 44. *See also* diffusion of innovations theory; innovation
advertising departments: Craigslist as competition, 9, 13; news departments' relationship with, 50, 55–57; revenue dropping in, 13–14; social media building revenues for, 49, 72; targeting audiences, 8
agenda setting, xiii, 55, 58–60, 74
Ahmad, Ali Nobil, 17
AJC.. *See Atlanta Journal-Constitution (AJC)*
Anderson, William, 53
Arceneaux, Noah, 18
Armstrong, Cory L., 18
arts critics, 62–63
Atlanta Journal-Constitution (AJC): about, 10–11; boundary expansion, 51–53; criticism of, 37; editor tweets, 23; financial pressures, 42; journalists' opinions of Twitter, 23, 32; personal interests in Twitter accounts, 51; quantity of tweets, 33; quotas for social media, 37; realigning teams, 78; sales of newspapers linked to Facebook, 49; staff specialists in social media, 56–57; uses of Twitter, 26, 48, 61–62, 64; website referrals linked to social media, 50

audience: connecting to, 66; engagement of, 17, 51–53; feedback from, 14; influencing media content, 8, 60; participating in news, 54; reader comments, 55; relationships with, 29, 77. *See also* followers
audience departments, 56
audiocassettes, 2
Aurora, Colorado shootings, xi, 57–58, 72

Barnard, Stephen R., 16
beat structure of newsrooms, 53
Beauion, Andrew, 17
Becker, Lee, 53
benefits of Twitter, 28–29. *See also* social capital
Benson, Rodney, 43–44
best practices of Twitter, 16, 40, 71
Blasingame, Dale, 18
Blaskovich, Sarah, 29, 48
Bluestein, Greg, 48, 64
Bonfils, F.G., 12
boundary theory in the newsroom: about, xii; advertising departments' relationships with reporters, 55–57; beat structure, 53; expanding role of journalists, 51–53; technology and boundary shifts, 54–55
Bourdieu, Pierre, 27, 43
Boyle, Kris, 16
branding through Twitter, 46–48, 69–70, 73, 77
breaking news: adding to social capital, 71; changes in timing of, 8, 57–58, 74; citizen journalism, 15; coverage of, 17; engagement in, 63–64; Facebook not suited for, 50; geographic reach of, 67–68, 71; immediacy of, 52; importance of,

About the Author

Alecia Swasy is the Donald W. Reynolds Chair in Business Journalism at Washington & Lee University. Previously, she was a reporter and editor at the Wall Street Journal, the St. Petersburg Times, and other publications. She is the author of *Soap Opera: The Inside Story of Procter & Gamble* and *Changing Focus: Kodak and the Battle to Save a Great American Company*, both published by Times Books/Random House. Swasy earned her doctorate and master's degrees from the Missouri School of Journalism, where she began the research for this book. She lives in Lexington, Virginia.